How to Flip Vacant Lots

How to Flip Vacant Lots

Break-Through Self-Funding Flip System

by

John Alexander

NuDay Publishing

Author's and Publisher's Legal Claims and Legal Disclaimers and Disclosures

Copyright © 2019
First Edition, 2019
Second Edition, 2020
Third Edition 2021
Fourth Edition 2023

The laws of various states vary in their requirements for attestation of a living trust and related documents.
THE DOCUMENTS USED OR PROVIDED IN THIS BOOK ARE FOR EXAMPLE USE ONLY AND SHOULD NOT BE COPIED OR REPRODUCED IN ANY MANNER FOR ONE'S PERSONAL USE. IT IS INTENDED AS AN ILLUSTRATION FOR YOUR UNDERSTANDING OF LIVING TRUSTS.

"This publication is designed to provide accurate and authoritative information in regard to the subject matter covered. It is sold with the understanding that the publisher is not engaged in rendering legal, accounting or other professional service. If legal advice or other expert assistance is required, the services of a competent professional person should be sought." From a Declaration of Principles jointly adopted by a committee of the American Bar Association and a committee of publishers and associations.

Use or the words and terms such as Best, Easiest, You Should, Fastest, Preferred, I recommend, etc., are all based on the author's opinion and not actual fact. They are used to convey the author's feelings about certain subject matter in the book.

ISBN: 9781093589634

Website links contained in the book may lead to affiliate websites in which the publisher earns a fee or commission for purchases made by the reader.

Copyright/Reproduction Information and Permissions for reprints may be requested from NuDay Publishing at www.johnalexander.com

DEDICATION

To my amazing son, living proof you can have the job you love and still flip real estate on the side to have the money you want.

Contents

HOW THE SELF-FUNDING SYSTEM WAS DISCOVERED	**10**
Resources for Real Estate Investors	17
SECTION 1	**18**
"THE SELF-FUNDING FLIP"	**18**
RULES OF THE LOT FLIPPING GAME TO LIVE BY	**19**
WHAT IS A VACANT LOT?	**20**
5-ACRES AND UP CAN STILL QUALIFY	**22**
THE SELF-FUNDING METHOD	**22**
MY SELF-FUNDING LAND FLIP FORMULA	**23**
RESEARCH THE AREA TO FIND TARGET LOTS OR TARGET SUBDIVISIONS	**24**
MAIL OUT TO THOSE OWNERS THAT FIT OUR CRITERIA	**25**
CALL THE OWNER BACK WITH A CASH OFFER	**26**
Magic of the Double Close	28
SELLER SCRIPT	**30**
THAT'S IT! IT'S TOO SIMPLE!	**32**
MY RECOMMENDED CRM SYSTEM	**33**
SECTION 2	**35**
FLIP DOCUMENTS AND LEGAL PROCEDURE	**35**
HOW TO DEAL IN REAL ESTATE IF THERE ARE LIENS OR JUDGMENTS FILED AGAINST YOU	**36**
UNDERSTANDING THE DEED	**37**
Parts of a Deed	37
WARRANTY DEEDS AND SPECIAL WARRANTY DEEDS	**42**
The "With All Faults" Clause	43
Warranty Deed Verses Special Warranty Deed Verbiage	45
Buy with a Warranty Deed, Sell with a Special Warranty Deed	46
Warranty Deed with Vendor's Lien	48
Understanding the Use of Names on Deeds	48
Joint Tenants and Tenants-in-Common	50
Creating Legal Documents without "Practicing Law" Issues	52

Married Couples and Community Property Signing Rules.................................54
HOW TO BUY PROPERTIES ALREADY IN A TRUST.................54
CREATING A GENERAL WARRANTY DEED...............................58
CREATING A SPECIAL WARRANTY DEED 61
HOW TO DO YOUR OWN CHAIN OF TITLE SEARCH 63
Similar Name Lien Issues 68
Deed of Trust Liens..69
Missing Names of Sellers in the Clerk's Records..70
Finishing up the Deed after the Search 74
How to Correct Legal Documents Before and After Filing 75
DINING-ROOM TABLE CLOSING 78
How to Self-close with Sellers 79
How to Self-Close with Buyers 81
HOW JUDGMENTS AND LIENS CAN BE OVERCOME 84
Offer to Buy the Lien at a Discount...85
Bankruptcy Issues..88
How to Double Close in a Title or Lawyer Office 90
BONUS SECTION 92
Summary 94
BOOKS BY JOHN ALEXANDER 97
ABOUT THE AUTHOR 103

HOW THE SELF-FUNDING SYSTEM WAS DISCOVERED

This book was written specifically for people with no experience in flipping property. It will provide you with my core discovery that revolutionized the land flipping industry, called the "Self-Funding Flip," complete with the exact steps and methods I perfected over the last 10 years of exclusively flipping land. In Section 2 of this book, I cover the more advanced information you can use to eliminate title companies and close your own land flips.

This book teaches you my self-funding flip method in a similar way to how I learned land flipping over 35 years ago. I learned it from my dad, who had a 3rd grade education and couldn't read or write except for his name. Despite this, he was able to run a business. He learned by someone telling him how to do something, and that's how he taught me. Now, I'm going to use written words to "tell" you how to do this business. Think of this as us having a conversation rather than just reading this book.

Within about 10 minutes of my dad giving me a quick overview and a phone number of a landowner, he set into motion something that continues to this day. Vacant lots are far easier to flip than any other form of real estate. I love a challenge, and within a few years of my father teaching me the land business, I went on to build homes, buy and fix, manage rentals, work in commercial real estate, establish a mortgage brokerage, and achieve national fame teaching hundreds of thousands of people how to flip homes.

My father lived 500 miles away from me. Ten years ago, my dad and I were having a conversation about a lot he was flipping. Two weeks later, he passed away at the age of 89. He enjoyed flipping these lots, so I thought it might be a good way to say goodbye to him by flipping a lot near me, as a remembrance of how we flipped land together so long ago. It was something he would have gotten a kick out of. To my surprise, it was a great bonding moment in my own heart, not being able to see him before he passed away. It also reawakened the feelings and passion I still had, all these years later, for flipping vacant lots. I suddenly understood why my father transitioned from creating large developments to flipping single vacant lots and small acreages over the years.

It gives you the freedom to do what you really love and want to do, and it gives you your time back. Freedom to live and not just work at the demands of others. It also sustained him, as it has me, well past his retirement years, never having to depend on a single source of income that could be taken away or could "run out" at any moment. It's my wish that it can do the same for you and your family. True long-term security comes with learning this method of flipping. If an 89-year-old man in a wheelchair who couldn't read or write can do it, anyone can.

The process is virtually stress-free when compared to fix and flips or even wholesaling, where you have a different level of workload, including the competition and seller drama that follows those kinds of deals. And now, as we slip into a falling housing market and a recession, house flippers are finding fewer and fewer deals and more and more competition. I'm not knocking other types of flips, but after being in that game for a long time, as I have, one enjoys slowing down the pace without giving up the same amount of profit.

To my surprise, I found that I can earn virtually the same amount flipping vacant lots "stress-free," with little to no competition trying to undercut my price as they do in wholesaling a house. I can also eliminate having to deal with many of the new laws limiting how and what you can say and do as a wholesaler in states that continue to pass statutes and make claims against wholesalers. Look, states have a valid point; many wholesalers simply don't receive a good enough education before entering into a contract with an owner and then completely dropping the ball with sellers.

Real estate often takes time to learn, and in my opinion, it is far better to begin with the simplest of transactions, which, to me, is flipping small vacant lots. Unlike homes, lots usually only need a single page to transfer ownership, much like a car title. Doesn't that sound simpler than the mountain of paperwork associated with flipping a house? We don't even need to inspect the land; I can tell you with certainty that it has dirt, bushes, and maybe some trees—all in great shape, or at least in good enough shape to sell.

Your basic paperwork consists of a deed to buy the lot and a deed to resell the lot to someone else. That's essentially the business in a nutshell. Mix in a little online marketing, and you have 90% of the business. The final 10% is finding the lots using the same means I did many years ago: the tax roll. And today, it's much easier to use tax roll information via computers and software that didn't exist when I started.

With these additional sources, it made something that was more difficult back then, far easier today. Every time I flip a lot these days, it gives me a memory shot of those great memories I had flipping lots with my dad. It feels like he's standing right there beside me with a smile on his face as we file that final deed on each flip.

Much of what I share in this book was learned as a result of flipping many lots all over my home state of Texas. It has been an education, involving a lot of learning and tweaking. I had to learn exactly what works today, what doesn't work, what never to do, and what always to do. The vacant lot business is similar to home flipping but is definitely different in some very important ways. You are about to receive all that valuable education for the cost of this book.

But hey, I built a multi-million-dollar business on perfecting the art of running headlong into brick walls and then figuring out a better way around them. Failure is a sure path to success, but if someone else has already gone through the pain and failure, why not pick their brain and avoid having to make the same mistakes while also getting a proven method that they finally figured out? Who knows, it might also work for you too.

As a business warning, let's start by being realistic. Flipping lots or even running any business isn't for everyone. Some of you will go out there, follow exactly what I detail here, and still end up with a big fat zero when it comes to making the business work. It simply isn't going to work out for some people. Why? Because nothing does—gym memberships, dating, online marketing; the failure rate is somewhere above 95%. People quit; they quit early, and they quit often. And it's a good thing for those of us who don't. It's how you make it to the 1%. It's not that the 1% is special; it's that the 99% won't put in the effort.

Greater minds than mine figured out long ago that there is a distribution model of success in almost any endeavor, and it applies to almost everything. Less than 2% will stick with that gym membership for the long haul. Less than 2% will become a millionaire before 30. It basically explains why we have the 1% at the top in just about everything. One in 100 people will earn over 350k in America. That's the 1% everyone is talking about. For every hundred cars you pass today, one of those owners will earn that kind of money. But the good news is, look how many cars you will pass or pass you on any given day, every day. That's a lot of people earning a lot of money, and nothing is stopping you from joining that huge club.

This distribution model is nothing new; it didn't just happen recently because of this President or that President, or this job market or that economic meltdown; it has always existed. Even back to the Roman Empire and before that, the Ancient Greeks. It happens everywhere and in everything. There is usually one or two students in a graduating class per 100 that are really gifted when it comes to learning. They make up the top person of that 2% or so, the valedictorian.

So how does this help you? It tells you something about what you have to do to achieve success in anything. It tells you that 100 people will try this and any other endeavor, and that 99 will quit too early. See, this isn't like the class valedictorian where you needed to be born with a gift that can't be obtained any other way. It is simply sticking to learning the process longer than the 99 other people who quit before they reached success.

And really, it's not even that hard, as 50% of people who try something new will stop within minutes or a couple of hours of starting. Another 20% will stop within a few days, and another 10 will stop within a week. That means you just have to outdistance those people by sticking with it for 2 or 3 months to get all the moving parts down pat, and you suddenly have sky-high confidence and a working knowledge of exactly what you have to do each week to make sure you are flipping X number of vacant lots to generate Y amount of income.

One of the natural fears people have when starting this or any business is the "fear of failure," which may include looking bad in front of family or friends, appearing ignorant to sellers or buyers, or getting into legal issues.

Just recognize these as normal fears everyone has when starting in this business. In fact, everyone who currently flips property has those same fears, but it hasn't stopped the hundreds of thousands of investors flipping property every month in America, so it shouldn't stop you either. We can and will look at things to help keep us within the legal lines, leaving the fear of failing as the most problematic issue for people just starting up a business.

I found the best way to handle that is to keep your new business under wraps until you get that first check in your hands. Then it's hard for loved ones to warn you away from your business dream. I found the reason why our own loved ones give us a warning not to do something risky, like starting a business, is because if you fail, they feel bad for not warning you. They will also feel bad when they see the projected failure they fear you will have to endure.

This is why it's rare that we are born to parents who are risk-takers themselves and have no issue advising their children to go out and take risks as well. Human nature teaches us that this isn't how "good" parents should raise children. But, is it? You get the point;

don't blame them for shutting you down every time you want to take a risk. It's part of their job description to do that. It's called being a family member who is looking out to protect you.

Part of your job is to understand which kind of parent or friend you have and deal with them appropriately. Sometimes, that means keeping them in the dark about your new business enterprise.

Resources for Real Estate Investors

Other Books by John Alexander:

https://johnalexander.com

Advanced Mastermind for Land Flipping:

https://thealexandersecret.com

Basic Video Course on Land Flipping:

https://landmogul.com

Join our Vacant Lot Flipping Facebook Group:

https://facebook.com/groups/landmogul

SECTION 1

"THE SELF-FUNDING FLIP"

RULES OF THE LOT FLIPPING GAME TO LIVE BY

1. Never put-up earnest money on a lot flip transaction. Using my Self-Funding System will result in you never having to risk or spend earnest money with your offers. A contract requires only "mutual promises" as the "consideration" to make a legally binding contract. Seller promises to sell, and buyer promises to buy is a mutual promise.

2. Never let a buyer move onto or start clearing a property before you have closed with the seller and buyer, thus having all parties paid.

3. Never make promises or guarantees to a seller or a buyer.

4. Always use a purchase agreement in every transaction.

5. Everything must be in writing in the world of real estate.

6. Never advertise for buyers without having a property under contract.

7. Never charge buyers upfront fees.

8. Don't offer "Services" to Buyers or Sellers. You are an investor, not a real estate agent.

· Don't let other people talk you out of your business. We use a double close method, not a wholesaling method.

WHAT IS A VACANT LOT?

Before we can get you to the point of flipping vacant lots, we need to define what one is and why we flip vacant lots rather than other types of vacant land. The vacant lots I flip and teach others to flip using the self-funding method are usually found in an existing subdivision and have a value under $30,000. I have other methods taught elsewhere that are designed for lots and land greater than $30,000.

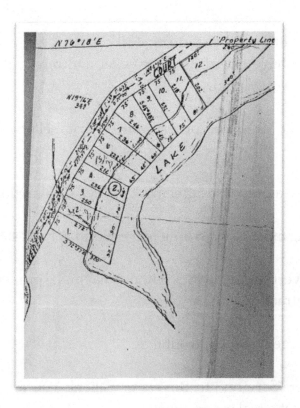

A subdivision is a large parcel of land that has been formally developed to some point by a developer who installed roadways and platted lots along those roadways. They are often referred to as "infill" lots.

Each lot has a similar feel to it in that they tend to repeat exactly the same dimension or close to the same dimension or acreage size. For example, current laws dictate the minimum size a lot can be in a given area. Most of these subdivisions have lots typically starting at 0.10 (tenth) of an acre up to 1 acre. Other subdivisions can have lots up to 10 acres, but these are rare.

Other attributes like the installation of paved streets, curbs, water, and sewer systems may be required as well. Because of this, we can see from a Google Map overhead view, very tight clumps of homes or lots and homes that fit into subdivisions. Some subdivisions will have 30 lots, and some will have hundreds or thousands of lots.

One can work a subdivision (flipping lots) with 2,000 lots for years if even 10% are still vacant. Most of the subdivisions that have great deals to flip have fewer than 300 lots total. And I've flipped in subdivisions as small as 20 lots. However, you will often find at least a few deals in almost any subdivision where homes have been built, or where mobile homes have been placed.

The idea here is that size doesn't matter when flipping vacant lots, but something else far more important does: the motivation level of the owner. I may find a huge subdivision but find only one lot from a single owner that responds to that mailing. Then later, another responds. The more I mail, the more I uncover, but they are really only responding in "their own" time, not mine. A lot owner doesn't put as much importance on the lot as other things they have going on in their life, so they will respond only when their life lines up with their wanting to take care of that now. This is why repeated mailing works far better with land than it does with homes.

I may also find that a smaller subdivision has a larger number of great leads, which means the owner lives farther away, across the state, or even out of the state. What matters in the end is this: Is there a vacant lot in the subdivision, and how far away does the owner live? I love out of county or out of state owners the best. The further away the owner lives, the better chances of you getting a great deal on it.

5-ACRES AND UP CAN STILL QUALIFY

While 1 acre or less is our general definition of a vacant lot, this doesn't mean we are limited to these sizes. We can flip any size parcel, but we would need to utilize different methods once we get above lots that we retail for over $20,000.

This means there are plenty of 5 to 10-acre parcels that can be flipped using the same methods we use to flip smaller lots, but you will need to find acres in the $1,000 per acre price range to purchase and use this method. Most acreage near big cities is far greater in price and won't work with this method. You will need to look further away to find them in the lower price range. It is the pricing structure that dictates our limits with the core self-funding methods you will learn in this book.

THE SELF-FUNDING METHOD

In 2013, I created a method of flipping vacant lots that I call "The Self-Funding Flip." It uses the buyer's Earnest Money Deposit (EMD) to actually pay for the lot. It works very similarly to a "Double Close" in that we are using money from the buyer being held in the closing process to fund the purchase. However, this closing can take about a week or two to complete.

Here's the formula for using the "end buyer's" deposit money (earnest money) to buy the lot from the seller and then double-closing the deal

MY SELF-FUNDING LAND FLIP FORMULA

1. Find a Lot.

2. Research it.

3. Contract to buy the lot from the seller at normally 25% to 50% of market value.

4. Market the lot, usually using a "For Sale" sign or Facebook Marketplace.

5. Contract to sell the lot to a buyer at 80 to 90% of market value, and for all cash; during hot markets, you can sell for full market value. (Advanced methods outside this book get into owner financing).

6. Take in the Deposit (earnest money) from the buyer that equals the price we contracted to buy the lot from the Seller.

7. Use the EMD deposit to pay and close with the seller using the notary method taught later in this book. Draw up the deed using the methods taught later in the book.

8. Close with the buyer, obtaining the balance of the purchase price. Draw up your own deed and file it directly with the County Deed of Records office.

9. This is a formula that rarely changes in concept, even though you could say every deal is different. You will see this constant formula at work in the overall process in every vacant lot flip.

RESEARCH THE AREA TO FIND TARGET LOTS OR TARGET SUBDIVISIONS.

Use the county appraisal office's online GIS map or commercially available GIS apps for mobile devices to locate target vacant lots in existing subdivisions. I recommend the Team subscription version at **https://regrid.com**. It offers the best-priced list available since it provides all the properties in any given area of interest. It also allows you to look at the property for flood zones, topography, and measure the lot, among other features. You can even save the searched area.

We are looking for vacant "tree-filled" or "empty" lots inside existing subdivisions filled with homes. Once located, click on the lot to find the owner's name and mailing address. If it is out of the area or out of state, then that becomes a target property we will mail a letter to, requesting to buy it for cash. It's easier to locate empty lots by turning off the satellite view and just using the map view, as this view usually draws 2D house shapes onto the lot.

This makes it easy to see the ones without homes. The satellite view is more difficult due to trees blocking rooftops. I've marked vacant lots in the screenshot below. Most GIS maps allow you to double-click on the individual lot to obtain the mailing address of the owner. This means out-of-state or out-of-area owner's contact information is built into the GIS system. You can then download entire mailing lists for additional sorting based on price, size, location of the owner versus the property, etc.

MAIL OUT TO THOSE OWNERS THAT FIT OUR CRITERIA.

Mail out a letter asking if the seller is interested in selling the lot to you for cash and a fast closing. We have this letter already written for you in the Files Section if you are part of our free Land Mogul Facebook group area. If not, join right now at: **http://facebook.com/groups/landmogul** Send out about 20 to 50 letters per week at most; any more than that, and you can overwhelm yourself with seller responses and miss opportunities had you paced yourself.

We take calls from owners and ask to get back later with an offer. We RESEARCH the lot and ownership using methods taught later in this book.

You want to find answers to the following questions about each before you give the Seller your Offer:

1. What is the address, legal description, or Assessor's Parcel Number (APN)?
2. Lot size either by acreage or square footage?
3. Dimensions of the property (see GIS map below or the appraiser's record)?
4. Are there improvements on the property; home, mobile home, etc.?
5. Do any improvements still exist?
6. Are there utilities on the property or in front of the property, gas, water, septic, well, utility pole hook-up, water lines, water tap?
7. What is the tax assessed value?
8. Are there any title issues from a title search you initially performed?
9. Does the county have online assessment or parcel maps also known as GIS maps?
10. If so, how can you access the online map or in-office maps?
11. What are the values of nearby properties?
12. What are the properties on all sides used for?
13. What are the properties in this subdivision selling for?
14. Have there been any recorded sales or listings of current for-sale lots on Zillow.com, Redfin.com, or Realtor.com nearby?

CALL THE OWNER BACK WITH A CASH OFFER

To determine the amount of the offer, use the above steps to determine what other lots have sold for, either in this subdivision or in the immediate area. Take that average price and divide it in half. Then using this new 50% number, our offer should be half of that number but can be as much as 60% if the area is "hot", or 25% or less if the area or subdivision is in a lesser desired area. To determine if the area is hot, look at the sales activity in this subdivision or immediate area. This means that your typical cash offer to most sellers will be 25% to as high as 60% of the typical sales price recorded on Zillow as Sold or Listed Price.

Our Written Offer Once a seller accepts our offer, we draw up a purchase contract and mail it to the seller for signature. We use a standard 1-page sales contract also called a purchase. We never use earnest money in my transaction with the seller.

Once we receive the purchase agreement back, we file a memorandum of it with the county clerk deed of records. (We provide our members with access to my documents such as the offer contract, memorandum, deeds, trusts, and more using my autofill online software. Get access at **http://LandMogul.com**)

Place a For Sale sign on the Lot with your phone number. Create an ad and start marketing on Facebook Marketplace. Instruct interested buyers to visit the lot before negotiating the price. Meet interested buyers locally to negotiate and sign a purchase contract. Take in $3,000 up to $10,000 (½ of the full cash purchase amount) they agree to pay for the lot AS EARNEST MONEY. Arrange closing two weeks from that date.

Arrange with a notary local to the seller to meet the seller for notarizing signatures on a deed we provide, closing statement, and payment from us via a cashier's check for the purchase amount we agreed to buy the lot for.

Once you receive the deed back from the seller and notary, file the deed with the County Clerk's office. See their website for filing fees. Deeds can also be mailed into the clerk's office with the fee and filed by mail. Use tracking if you use the mail. I like using FedEx or UPS to avoid lost mail issues.

Call the Buyer to arrange Closing with them, usually at the County Clerk's office. But I've closed at Starbucks and my own home. If the buyer or land is far away, you can use a notary to handle the closing. Take in the final balance they owe, usually half of the purchase price, sign the closing statement, and file the deed with the clerk's office. Done, rinse and repeat over and over.

Magic of the Double Close

A closing process called a "Double Close" along with the "amounts" we are dealing with makes my Self-Funding Flip Formula work.

Like most of the ideas I have discovered in my flipping career, this one I stumbled into as I was doing land flips the "normal" way, by coming out of pocket with the purchase money or borrowing the money to close with the seller.

This is because initially, I would only ask buyers for $1,000 or $2,000 at most as an earnest money deposit. Since I don't normally use title companies with this method, I realized that I had full control of the money being given to me. I'm not a licensed escrow officer or company, so I don't have to follow their guidelines with how I handle the money.

What I found over the years is that you can ask and get even higher earnest money deposits. Just "require" that amount because you want to ONLY WORK WITH SERIOUS BUYERS. That's the excuse to ask for up to $10,000 earnest money deposits. Let's dive into this a little deeper so you can see this concept at work.

Let's set up the framework for what you are doing at this point in the transaction. If I were selling you a used car that you loved and wanted more than anything and that car had a market value of $20,000; and I asked you to put up $1,000 as a deposit and pay the rest at closing, that would be a normal deal and all would go smoothly. But if I asked you to put up $10,000, you might say no because you can go buy that same used car from someone else who is offering it at the same price but with a $1,000 deposit.

Now let's change just the price alone and see what happens. If I were selling you the same $20,000 car but now, I'm asking just

$12,000 as the sale price but require a $6,000 deposit, would you take that deal or would you rather find a different seller who would sell you the same car with a $1,000 deposit... but you had to pay $20,000 for that one? Which deal would you buy right now if you needed and wanted that car? Only a crazy person would pay double the price just because of the deposit size. That money goes to pay for the car anyway. So how do we get buyers into the mood of putting up a larger earnest money deposit?

So, in the Self-Funding Flip Formula, the larger earnest money deposit serves multiple purposes:

- It demonstrates the buyer's serious commitment to the deal.
- It allows you, as the investor, to fund the purchase of the lot from the seller without having to come up with the money yourself or borrowing it.
- It provides a safety net in case either you or the buyer needs to cancel the deal.

When you ask for a larger deposit from the buyer, remember to emphasize that they are getting a great deal on the property at a significantly discounted price compared to the market value. Most buyers will understand the reasoning behind the higher deposit and be willing to commit to it, knowing they are getting a good deal.

In the rare case that a buyer pushes back on the deposit amount, you can explain that the larger deposit ensures their commitment to closing the deal and helps you move forward with confidence. If they still have concerns, you can ask them if the issue is related to the deposit amount or their decision to purchase the property.

With the Self-Funding Flip Formula, you can use the buyer's deposit to purchase the lot from the seller and complete the transaction. In the event that the deal falls through on either side, the deposit can be returned to the buyer or used as compensation for breach of contract, depending on the situation.

This innovative approach to flipping vacant lots not only streamlines the process but also minimizes your financial risk as an investor, making it an attractive option for those looking to build a successful land flipping business.

Therefore, there are almost no situations where I could get into a legal bind by using the earnest money to make the purchase. However, there might be some situations that would prevent you from completing it with that reason being your fault; you might have a heart attack, be in a severe accident, die, or other extreme situations which could cause you to fail to close out the transaction with the buyer.

Even so, you may still be able to have someone else close it out for you, including a local attorney. More on using closing attorneys later.

Looking at the worst-case scenario, as I like to do with buyers and sellers, you could have purchased the property, failed to close with the seller, meaning you didn't use the earnest money, so now you simply return it to the buyer.

How many times has that happened to me over the 5 years I've been using this technique? Never, not once. And after you do a few deals, you will have an understanding that it would be almost impossible to end up in that worst-case scenario, and if you did, your problems are a lot worse than owing someone a few thousand dollars.Seller Script

When a seller/owner calls you from a mailing, the conversation will go something like this:

Yes, I'm still interested in buying your lot. Are you looking for a cash price or are you willing to owner finance it? (If the lot is already super cheap, skip the above and just say you are "still interested in buying the lot.") What is your name? What county is the property in? What is the name listed on the deed? Is it yours, you and another person, or just you by yourself? Ok, let me do this: I'm going to pull up the records on the lot so I can refresh my memory on this one, and I'll give you a call tomorrow with my offer. Will that work for you?

The next day, you will call the owner back, having researched the property and coming up with a price that fits our Self-Funding Model.

"Mr. Smith, I've looked over everything and can make you a cash offer. You won't need to come here to close; I'll pay for all the closing costs and the survey. If you like my offer, I'll pay you in the form of a certified check and can deliver it to you by my notary at your home. I've been buying lots here in the $4,000 to $6,000 range. I like your lot, so my cash offer is $6,000.00." If you haven't yet bought anything, say, "Lots like yours seem to be selling in the $4k to $6k range."

At this point, they will usually say yes or no. If they express a no, then follow up with, "I wish I could offer you more, but that's the current cash value lots are selling for here." Then go over the facts you discovered in your research that would show that's the cash value today.

Normally, I won't negotiate with the seller at all, nor do they negotiate with you. It is always a yes or no, but you can change a no to a yes by showing them what other properties have sold for or the fact that no properties can be found having sold, showing that a lack of demand is an issue.

If a seller says yes, then you will cover the steps that will follow. You will mail out the contract, and when you're ready to close, you'll arrange with a local notary to meet the seller at their bank. (This process is detailed in a later chapter.)

I normally use a simple one-page purchase contract and will mail it to the seller for signatures. While sometimes you could email it, you actually want extra time to go by while you start the sales process on the property.

From the seller's standpoint, they would usually send the contract to the closing attorney to have the deed and closing statement drawn up. They don't know the turnaround time for that but assume it will take a few weeks. By that time, you should have the property sold and ready to finish the closing process, detailed later in this book.

THAT'S IT! IT'S TOO SIMPLE!

I just went over the nuts and bolts of my basic system for flipping these self-funding vacant lot flips. The mechanics of other parts of the transaction not covered in this book, such as negotiating, ads, etc., are similar to any other part of any real estate transaction that you can learn on YouTube. Don't make this harder than it is. However, I do break down every step in two places.

The remaining part of this book will deal with the legal aspects of the deal, including the deed, title closings, etc.

If you would like to learn all my various flip methods that I've developed to flip land of all sizes and at all prices, including very advanced owner finance methods, consider joining my program.

This includes weekly Zoom calls with me going into detail about exactly what is working in today's market and answering all your questions live.

From beginners to home wholesalers, now is the time to stop the grind and start flipping lots.

MY RECOMMENDED CRM SYSTEM

As your business grows, you'll find that you need more organization and automation to allow your deal flow to grow while maintaining the time freedom you started the business to achieve for you and your family. I have used many CRMs over the years and found that the best one to use and at the time of this printing, costs only $97 per month. It not only provides a cutting-edge CRM, but also has many other features built into it, such as websites, email system, SMS, voiceless ring drops, Facebook integration, and an automated text follow-up system to continue reaching out to sellers and buyers until they are ready to act. A huge bonus is the networking with other land flipping members who share help and even JV opportunities. Here's the link to get you started:

Http://LeadMachinePlus.com

Remember, investing in the right tools can significantly improve your efficiency and effectiveness in managing your land flipping business, allowing you to scale up and enjoy the time freedom you desire.

SECTION 2

FLIP DOCUMENTS AND LEGAL PROCEDURE

HOW TO DEAL IN REAL ESTATE IF THERE ARE LIENS OR JUDGMENTS FILED AGAINST YOU

Over the years, many people have asked me if they can still flip property even if they have liens, judgments, or even IRS liens filed against them. While having a lien, judgment, or garnishment filed against you may prevent you from owning future property, using a trust can be a solution to this problem.

By having someone else be named as the trustor in your trust and you as the trustee, you can bypass any "ownership" issues. You don't own the property; the trustor owns the property. As the trustee, you act more like a manager who is allowed to sign their name on documents.

This means you can operate your real estate business no matter how challenging life has been for you in the past. Your trustor could be your spouse, a family member, or a close friend. Remember, the person you are today is not the same as the person you were in the past; it's the person you are about to become in the future.

We now turn to the "legal" side of this business – the "Rule Book," if you will. The first step in winning any game is understanding what the rules are. The person who knows the rules is usually very good at winning the game.

UNDERSTANDING THE DEED

Understanding how deeds work and how they are created is important, as we often need to draw them up ourselves. Initially, you may use an online service, but you will quickly find that it is the same document with only a few changing parts. Therefore, you will likely end up drawing them up yourself once you learn how. This chapter aims to teach you most of what you need to know to draw them up yourself while learning about the document.

Deeds are used to transfer ownership from one person to another. They serve as the "Title" to the property. The process for selling a property involves creating a deed from the existing owner to the new owner.

The deed is filed with the county clerk's office in the county where the property is located. Deeds are documents that follow the traditional structure used in that state, providing numerous examples of how to draw up your own deed if you are not closing with a title company or attorney.

Note: California uses a grant deed instead of a General Warranty Deed in most transfers. Some versions of the grant deed have a written warranty, while others do not, but they all convey ownership.

First, we will cover what you need to understand about deeds; then, we will move into using a trust to hide our name from lawsuit happy lawyers when the deed is drawn up, whether you are creating them yourself or a closing agent is having the deed drawn up by an attorney.

Parts of a Deed

Deeds are indeed quite simple documents, with their structure remaining largely unchanged since early America. A deed contains five basic parts:

1. The first part of a deed is where the parties are named and assigned the positions of Grantor and Grantee. The Grantor is the seller, and the Grantee is the buyer, with traditional legal terms such as "Convey, Bargain, Grant, and/or Sell" placed in the text to indicate the transfer of property from one party to another. A date when the sale occurred is stated, and "consideration" (a thing of value) is shown, which is a requirement of all deeds. This is usually shown as a token amount of money, such as ten dollars, but could also be expressed as "For Valuable Consideration." Never place the full amount of money paid for property in a deed.

2. The second part describes the land by legal description, which defines the location of the land being sold by describing the physical measurements or location of the property in that county.

3. The third part describes any reservations or hold-outs, such as gas and oil rights. It often reads that the deed is "subject to" these reservations.

4. The fourth part describes how the Grantor will warranty (also known as "guarantee") that they own the property free and clear of any liens or claims and will defend their title should anyone make a claim of ownership or lien against the property now or in the future.

5. The fifth part is where the Grantor (seller) has their signature notarized, proving that the person is who they say they are and the date on which they signed. Notice that the Grantee does not have to sign anywhere on the deed. This is a powerful detail that allows for creativity in other areas of this book. The only person who must sign the deed is the current owner. If the property is held in a trust, then the trustee would be the only one signing the deed.

Now that we've covered the five basic parts of a typical warranty deed, you should have a better understanding of how a deed is structured and be more comfortable with the document.

NOTICE OF CONFIDENTIALITY RIGHTS: IF YOU ARE A NATURAL PERSON, YOU MAY REMOVE OR STRIKE ANY OR ALL OF THE FOLLOWING INFORMATION FROM THIS INSTRUMENT BEFORE IT IS FILED FOR RECORD IN THE PUBLIC RECORDS: YOUR SOCIAL SECURITY NUMBER OR YOUR DRIVER'S LICENSE NUMBER.

WARRANTY DEED

THAT I, **R. Ross Mason Jr. and wife Mary Anne Mason**, hereafter referred to as **Grantor**, whose address is 419 Main St 779, Grady, TX 76642, whether one or more, for and in consideration of the sum of TEN AND NO/100 ($10.00) DOLLARS and other good and valuable consideration to the undersigned paid by the Grantee herein named, the receipt of which is hereby acknowledged, have GRANTED, SOLD AND CONVEYED, and by these presents do GRANT, SELL AND CONVEY unto the John Alexander, Trustee for the **Dallas 5883 Trust**, referred to as "**Grantee**," whose address is 63 Woodberry, Dallas, Texas 76644, all of the following described real property in Dallas County, Texas, to-wit:

Legal Description:
Lot 5, Block 8, in Southfork Subdivision, according the the Maps and Plat records in Vol 445, Page 44, filed in Dallas County TX. APN. 008840030004

This conveyance is made subject to any and all reservations of oil, gas and minerals, and valid exceptions, covenants, conditions and restrictions contained in the chain of title of said premises, including sales or reservations of oil, gas and minerals; now of record in the County Clerk's office of DALLAS County, Texas, but only to the extent they are still in force and effect.

TO HAVE AND TO HOLD the above described premises, together with all and singular the rights and appurtenances thereto in anywise belonging, unto the said grantee, his heirs and assigns forever, and we do hereby bind myself, my heirs, executors and administrators, to WARRANT AND FOREVER DEFEND all and singular the said premises unto the said grantee, his heirs and assigns, against every person whomsoever lawfully claiming or to claim the same or any part thereof.

EXECUTED this _____ day of _____ , 20_____

_____
R. Ross Mason, Jr

_____
Mary Anne Mason

THE STATE OF **TEXAS** §
COUNTY OF _____ §

This instrument was acknowledged before me on this _____ day of _____, 20___
by **R. Ross Mason, Jr. and wife Mary Anne Mason.**

_____

The warranty deed above shows a typical married couple who owned a property in their personal names, conveying the property to one of my trusts that I use as an investor. Below is an example of how it would look if a couple owned a property in their family trust and were conveying it to my trust. In this case, it will be one trust/trustee conveying to another trust/trustee.

WARRANTY DEED

THAT I, **Tom Smith and wife Rose Smith, Co-Trustees for the Smith Family Trust**, hereafter referred to as **Grantor**, whose address is 419 Turkey St 779, Grady, TX 76642, whether one or more, for and in consideration of the sum of TEN AND NO/100 ($10.00) DOLLARS and other good and valuable consideration to the undersigned paid by the Grantee herein named, the receipt of which is hereby acknowledged, have GRANTED, SOLD AND CONVEYED, and by these presents do GRANT, SELL AND CONVEY unto the **John Alexander, Trustee for the Dallas 5883 Trust**, referred to as "**Grantee**," whose address is 63 Woodberry, Dallas, Texas 76644, all of the following described real property in **Dallas** County, Texas, to-wit:

WARRANTY DEEDS AND SPECIAL WARRANTY DEEDS

A general warranty deed is the safest deed type to use for transferring property into the trust if the property is currently owned by a seller or party other than yourself. This is to keep them financially responsible for warranting/guaranteeing the title, from the past to the present. You want "good title," which means the chain of title is clear of liens or other claims.

If you are an investor and flipping this property, i.e., you are selling this property to a buyer, and you didn't buy a title insurance policy when you originally bought the property, then it is safer to use a special warranty deed for the transfer to limit your guarantee.

However, if you had purchased a title insurance policy on the property when you originally bought it, you shouldn't mind using a general warranty deed in the transfer. If there is a future title issue, you would be able to hold your title insurance company responsible for curing the claim.

My basic rule is to never give a general warranty deed if I didn't obtain title insurance when I bought the property; rather, I give a special warranty deed. This is because using a general warranty deed means I'm guaranteeing that I will pay off any and all claims that might be made against it since it was first deeded into existence.

A special warranty deed only requires you to warranty (guarantee) the title free and clear of all claims, from the date you bought it until the date you sold it. This means you don't warranty the title from anyone else or from any time before you owned it.

In your normal course of business as a real estate investor, you always want to take ownership (buy) with a general warranty deed (if possible) and sell using a special warranty deed (if possible), unless you bought a title insurance policy from a title company to protect you from claims from the past.

Therefore, when I sell property that is not going to be closed by a title company or title attorney, i.e., where we "self-close" the transaction, it means that I'm passing title to another without a title insurance policy in place.

When that happens, it is the choice of the buyer to accept the property without a title policy in place. This means that if an issue arises with the title, such as a missed lien, bankruptcy, old ownership claim, etc., I cannot be held legally or financially accountable as the seller since I didn't use a warranty deed to convey title.

To minimize my legal responsibility in deeds and property transfers where there is no title insurance policy purchased by any party, I will do two things. First, I will only convey title to a buyer using a special warranty deed. Second, I will always include a "With All Faults" clause in the deed to protect myself from other negative issues like boundary disputes, adverse possession claims, or issues with the land itself.

The "With All Faults" Clause

> GRANTOR MAKES NO REPRESENTATIONS OR WARRANTIES, EXPRESS OR IMPLIED, AS TO THE SUITABILITY OR FITNESS OF THE PROPERTY FOR ANY PURPOSE, OR AS TO THE VALUE, QUALITY OR CONDITION OF THE PROPERTY. THE SALE OF THE PROPERTY BY GRANTOR TO GRANTEE SHALL BE "AS IS", "WHERE IS", AND "WITH ALL FAULTS." THE FOREGOING PROVISIONS SURVIVE THE DELIVERY OF THIS DEED.

Let's look at why you would use this clause and the protections it affords you. What if the city steps in and condemns the property you just sold, or there is some back debt owed to the city, county, etc., that wasn't found in a title search? What if a bond or financial commitment is required to be put up in order to get some type of utility service? What if a permit wasn't pulled before the last owner put on a new addition? Or maybe, as in some areas of California, what if the water is bad or the wells have gone dry, but you didn't know that when you bought and quickly resold the property?

These are all unforeseen occurrences that can and do happen to people every day. Recently, in Houston, Texas, there were whole areas of the city that were not in a flood zone before a hurricane hit.

Now, thousands of properties are in a new flood zone, making many properties worthless or less than they were previously worth.

All these kinds of issues can be avoided by making sure your deed clears you of them. All a buyer has to do is make the claim you did know or should have known. They don't even have to be right to cost you money to defend yourself.

The special warranty deed states in the warranty section that the seller only guarantees that they personally haven't created any title issues, such as selling it to someone else or having placed/obtained a lien against it during the time they held ownership of the property.

This is different from a general warranty deed guarantee, where the seller warrants and will defend against anyone claiming an issue from the time the original parcel was created until the present. If you're not protecting yourself with a title policy, why would you take on that responsibility? You wouldn't, yet I see it happen all the time, needlessly.

A special warranty deed keeps you safe from title issues, and having a "With All Faults" clause like the one above keeps you from implying that the property is without other issues. Together, the two methods allow you to convey title exactly as you received it and help prevent ghosts from coming back to haunt you later.

Warranty Deed Verses Special Warranty Deed Verbiage

We just covered how the two deeds are different, now let's look at the actual wording to better understand how they look in their perspective deeds. This difference is found in the guarantee section of the deed.

Read each one of the following deed clauses and see if you can find the difference. They both look very similar but yield a big difference in what they claim you will warranty/guarantee.

A General Warranty Deed "Guarantee":

> TO HAVE AND TO HOLD the above described premises, together with all and singular the rights and appurtenances thereto in anywise belonging, unto the said grantee, his heirs and assigns forever, and we do hereby bind myself, my heirs, executors and administrators, to WARRANT AND FOREVER DEFEND all and singular the said premises unto the said grantee, his heirs and assigns, against every person whomsoever lawfully claiming or to claim the same or any part thereof.

A Special Warranty Deed "Guarantee":

> Grantor binds Grantor and Grantor's heirs, executors, administrators, successors and assigns to warrant and forever defend all and singular the Property to Grantee and Grantee's heirs, executors, administrators, successors, and assigns against every person whomsoever lawfully claiming or to claim the same or any part thereof, when the claim is by, through or under Grantor, but not otherwise, except as to the Reservations from Conveyance and the exceptions to Conveyance and Warranty.

The magic words in the special warranty deed are "Through or under Grantor, but not otherwise." Keep in mind that you are selling the property, so you are the grantor. This means that only the grantor's actions connected to the title are guaranteed and only while the grantor held the title. Therefore, while you, the grantor, are the owner of the title, you will defend against all claims, but not otherwise. This means that you will not defend and guarantee the title before you took ownership. As long as you do not get a lien against the trust, you should have no adverse claim issues regarding the chain of title while you hold the title on that property.

Buy with a Warranty Deed, Sell with a Special Warranty Deed

When selling a property, I only give a general warranty deed to someone who has purchased property from me if I previously purchased a title policy when I bought the property. Otherwise, I insist that I convey title at closing with a special warranty deed. If the buyer requires me to convey title with a warranty deed because they received some bad advice from someone,

I will only do so if the buyer pays for an "Owners Policy" for me. Usually, a good title closer can explain to them why it is unnecessary for me to convey with a general warranty deed. I do not care which way they want me to convey; I am just not paying for their lack of understanding or getting bad advice.

It is customary in some locations for one of the parties, buyer or seller, to pay for a title policy for the buyer. This policy is called an Owner's Title Policy, but you do not have to do what is customary. I do what is logical, and so should you. I am not spending money to protect someone else after they purchase from me, and if I use a special warranty deed with the "All Faults" clause, then I do not need protecting. The buyer should pay for their policy.

Now, let us look at the same issues when buying a property from a seller. Given all of the above, you will know why you want the seller to give you a general warranty deed when you buy a property. You want the last owner to fully guarantee the title for you when you buy, so always ask for a general warranty deed when you buy property.

However, be willing to take a special warranty deed if you had a title search done or are satisfied by your chain of title search. If you are holding the property long-term and not flipping it at closing, then you will want to buy a policy to protect yourself on higher valued properties.

If the property owner purchased a title insurance policy when they originally bought the property, that policy will act as their protection in case a title issue arises. However, if they did not purchase such a policy, then they will have to pay out-of-pocket to settle any claims that may arise.

As an investor, it is recommended to "buy" with a general warranty deed and "sell" with a special warranty deed. However, it is possible to buy a property where the owner is only using a special warranty deed to sell. This is particularly relevant when the property is being flipped, as the next owner can decide how they wish to warranty the title.

If ownership is split between people, or if it is a probate property that they inherited, the owners may prefer to convey the property by special warranty deed if they have spoken to a good attorney. In such cases, it is acceptable to accept a special warranty deed.

At the end of the day, any deed effectively passes ownership, and if added protection is needed, a title policy can always be purchased either by oneself or by the next owner.

It is not necessary to go through a closing with the title company to get the research done. Title companies or services like protitleusa.com can sell Title Abstracts (a chain of title search) for approximately $200, which will list any problems they find in the chain of title history.

It is also possible to pay for the abstract before purchasing a property, so that if everything is okay, a title company can issue a title policy. This saves on escrow fees and other costs that title companies may charge. On land lots, a title policy can cost as little as $300.00 to $500.00 at the time of this writing, meaning that a safe title closing can be pieced together for approximately $400 without using expensive escrow account services and other fees that can add up to $1000 or more even on small deals.

Warranty Deed with Vendor's Lien

A warranty deed, when paired with a deed of trust, is referred to as a "Warranty Deed with Vendor's Lien." This is used when a loan has been made to the buyer, and the lender places a lien against the property. When you see such a deed, look for either a deed of trust or a mortgage that was filed along with the warranty deed.

It is important to note that all the general ideas presented in this book can certainly be applied to property with loans against them. Once you complete a deal with an attorney, you should be able to handle subsequent deals by using your new knowledge found in this book.

Understanding the Use of Names on Deeds

At some point, you may come across a transaction where the seller has changed their name since they originally signed the deed years earlier, either through marriage or otherwise. In such cases, it is important to ensure that the new deed connects the correct names, like a daisy chain.

For example, if Paula Thomas was listed on a deed ten years ago as the owner, but she has since married and changed her name to Paula Brown, her photo ID needed for notary purposes will read "Paula Brown." To address this, her original name will be put into the proper area for grantor, and the words "Same Person As," "formerly known as," or "also known as" will be added, followed by her new name. It will look something like this: "Paula Thomas, Same Person As Paula Brown."

It is important to note that using a middle name or initial in one legal document and not using it in another typically does not create a question of identity affecting titles. However, it is best to consult with an attorney or title company for specific guidance on how to handle any name changes in the context of a particular transaction.

WARRANTY DEED

THAT I, **Paula A. Brown, same person as, Paula Thomas**, hereafter referred to as **Grantor**...

When it comes to the signature and notary area at the bottom of the document, it is important to use only the seller's current name, i.e., "Paula Brown," for signing and notary purposes. This is because they will not be able to verify their old name, as their ID card will only list their new name. It is also not necessary to use their old name for these purposes.

It is acceptable to leave out a middle initial, but it is important to try to be consistent with names throughout a single document. If "Sr." or "Jr." is used in one legal document, it must stay consistent in all subsequent legal documents. This is because title can be affected if this designation is left out or used inconsistently.

_____

Paula Brown, Signature

THE STATE OF **FLORIDA**

COUNTY OF JACKSON

This instrument was acknowledged before me on this _____ day of _____, 20___

by **Paula Brown**. _____

If you have questions about signature issues or other legal issues related to real estate transactions, you can always Google the question. There are plenty of answers available on the web. However, it is important to add the name of your state when searching legal questions, as laws and regulations can vary from state to state.

When naming married couples in real estate transactions, it is customary to include the fact that they are married. This is to automatically imply the legal benefits and other legal issues that go along with owning property as a married couple by state default.

Legal ways of naming parties in deeds:

> Thomas Wells and wife Lana Wells. ...

Same sex married couples can be name:

> Ted Wells and Bill Thompson, a married couple. ...

Buying from an Executor or Executrix, can be:

> Beth Thomas, Executrix for the Estate of Richard Thompson, ...

Buying from someone with Power of Attorney for another:

> Bart Smith, attorney in fact for Sean Ford Wallingford. ...

Buying from a couple, but the property was not obtained during the marriage or was inherited by only one them.

> John Smith, as his sole and separate property, herein referred to as Grantor... etc.

Joint Tenants and Tenants-in-Common

The following is something you can learn more about by doing some online research. It is not necessary, but it is nice to know. You do not need to advise buyers on how they should hold title, but it can be helpful when selling property to buyers who may be business partners or family members. This way, you can add an extension just after their names, such as "Joint Tenants with Rights of Survivorship" or "Tenants-in-Common."

It depends on what they want to happen to their share of the property should one of them pass away while still holding title

> Jeff McBride and Tim Caney, as Joint Tenants with Rights of Survivorship.

(Meaning when one dies, their half of the ownership automatically passes to the other person.)

Or...

> Jeff McBride and Tim Caney, as Tenants-in-Common.

If one of the property owners dies, their ownership passes to their legal heirs in the method of holding title called "Tenants-in-Common." This method of holding title can create a mess if the surviving owner is not comfortable with the deceased owner's family members who stand to inherit the property.

If you do not designate either choice, "Tenants-in-Common" is the default way that most states will rule when two people are listed on a deed who are not married, i.e., without the "Joint Tenants with Right of Survivorship" listed after their names. It is important to always use the words "with Right of Survivorship" after the term Joint Tenants, as without those words, most states will treat joint tenants much like they do tenants-in-common.

Creating Legal Documents without "Practicing Law"

Issues

While you cannot legally tell your buyer what to put into a deed or other legal document, as that would be giving legal advice, you can explain to them what each term means. They can then tell you what they want you to place in the deed.

As a party to the transaction, you can fill out any legal document in that transaction without practicing law without a license. In the situation above, you can start by saying that you cannot advise them on what to place after their name, but you can explain what each term means. Then, you can ask them how they want you to draw up the deed. For example, "Tenants-in-Common means this, and Joint Tenants means that. How do you want me to draw it up?"

It is important to ask what they want to place in the document rather than telling them or advising them what they should place in the document. This is a good rule to follow to avoid giving legal advice.

When a Trustee also Owns a Part of the Property

Another important "name designation" to be aware of is the word "Individually." This title should be added when someone is signing on behalf of another entity but also owns a part of the property themselves.

For instance, if a trust/trustee owns half of a property and the trustee owns the other half under their own name, then the signatures will have to reflect the same person signing either twice using their designation or once and using both designations in the signature area of the deed/document.

It is important to ensure that the signatures on the deed or other legal document reflect the correct ownership interests of all parties involved to avoid any potential issues with the ownership of the property.

Example:

> Sarah Smith, Individually, and as Trustee for the Smith Trust

Or

> Sarah Smith, Individually
>
> Sarah Smith, as Trustee for the Smith Trust

Married Couples and Community Property Signing Rules

Most states follow the same rules when it comes to having married couples sign deeds and other legal documents in real estate. Here are some important considerations:

1. If the property was conveyed to the couple while they were married, then both married persons must sign to reconvey the property.
2. If one of the couple obtained an inherited property or obtained property before the marriage and it was never comingled with their partner, then they alone can sign to convey the property.
3. Even if the other party of the marriage is not named on the last deed or document, have both husband and wife sign any deed to reconvey. This ensures that the community rights that the non-signing person has by default in the property are conveyed at closing, even if that person wasn't listed on the last deed.
4. In cases of divorce, if one party signed a Quit Claim deed to the other party, then that one party conveyed to in the Quit Claim can sign alone.

When the property of a married couple is conveyed, and it was inherited or owned before the marriage, then that property is referred to as their "Sole and Separate Property." This designation is also put on the deed following their name. For example, "John Smith, as his sole and separate property, herein referred to as Grantor... etc."

HOW TO BUY PROPERTIES ALREADY IN A TRUST

As an investor, you will come across properties that you wish to buy that are currently held in a trust. Let's explore how this happens and how to deal with these properties by understanding the necessary documents that must be in place before you can take title correctly.

For example, let's say you access the county deed records database and find a property listed as being owned by a trust. The following example shows how it may appear in California, where grant deeds are commonly used to convey property. In this case, the property is owned by a husband and wife who transferred their Texas property into a living trust in California. They are listed as trustees for the trust.

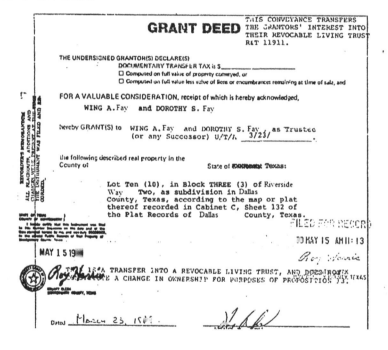

The following is how it may look in Texas and states that use warranty deeds to convey title.

GENERAL WARRANTY DEED

THIS INDENTURE, made as of November 10, 2017, between Joe Smith and Joyce Smith, whose address is 117 Main St. Dallas TX 75449. ("Grantor"), and Joe Smith and Joyce Smith as Trustees of the SMITH FAMILY TRUST, whose address is 117 Main St. Dallas TX 75449, ("Grantee").

WITNESSETH, that the Grantor(s), in consideration of Ten Dollars and other valuable consideration, the receipt and sufficiency of which is hereby acknowledged, do hereby transfer unto the Grantee and its heirs, executors, administrators, successors and assigns forever.

ALL that certain plot, piece or parcel of land, with the buildings and improvements thereon erected, situated, lying and being in the County of Dallas . and the State of Texas, being more particularly described as follows, to-wit:

SEE "EXHIBIT A" ATTACHED

In the top area of the deeds above, you will notice that the sellers are named and called the "Grantor." This means that those named are "granting" title of the property to the other party named as the "Grantee." You will also see that they have named themselves again as the grantee but in a trustee position.

For example, "Wing Fay and Dorothy Fay (with no designation as individuals) grants to Wing Fay and Dorothy Fay as trustee, the following property…etc." In the Texas property example above, a general warranty deed is used to convey property from Joe and Joyce Smith as grantors to Joe and Joyce Smith as trustees for the Smith Family Trust. In this deed, they provided the name of the trust as normally done but not required as seen in the previous example.

The deed is what transfers property into a trust so that the trustee of the trust legally holds the title to the property and not the trust name. Legal title is supposed to be held by a living person, not the actual trust. This is why, when properly done, the trustee is always named in the deed next to the name of the trust. When the time comes to resell or convey the property to another owner, everyone knows the name of the person (trustee) who will be transferring the property to the next party.

This is why title companies in states that don't use certifications of trusts normally insist on seeing the whole trust document, as they don't want to just take the word of the last trustee. Many states have statutes which force these third parties, such as title companies, to accept the certification of trust as the only document they are now allowed to see.

However, there are some natural problems you should be aware of with certifications of trusts since these problems help us hide our property, as later explained in this book. For example, during the time the trust held ownership of a property, the trustee may have been removed and replaced with another trustee. In that case, there most likely isn't any indication in public records of the switch to a new trustee.

But we don't concern ourselves with those kinds of issues outside of requiring they give us a certification of trust. We really protect ourselves with special warranty deeds and "With all Faults" clauses, so these issues are more of a concern for other, less informed people.

Because trustees can be switched out by the trustor, or a trustee can step down or even pass away, when a property held in a trust is resold or conveyed, a certification of trust should be filed by the trust, showing the then-current trustee, even if it is the same trustee listed on the original deed.

A certification of trust is filed by the current trustee as an affidavit that he/she is the current trustee of the trust. The trustee notarizes this document, and it is filed at the same time the deed is filed, transferring ownership to the new owners. Again, we see here that the trustor never shows up on public record, only the trustee is made public.

CREATING A GENERAL WARRANTY DEED

Most types of deeds can be used to convey property, but the ideal deed you should want others to use to convey to you is a general warranty deed. Ownership should go directly from the last owner to your entity, such as LLC or Living Trust, without going through your personal name first.

However, there will be times when this will be forced upon you. For example, if you are financing a property, the lender will often force you to complete the transaction in your personal name before allowing you to transfer it to your trust. This is so they can hold the person who applied for credit responsible for the loan, not a trustee. (See the section on equity-stripping to solve this issue.)

In this section, we will go over how to fill out a warranty deed when you are buying or taking ownership of a property in which there is no title company or closing attorney involved. In those cases, you will need to purchase a deed online or create one using the example deed provided. Once you know how to fill out one deed, it is pretty much the same way for any deed you choose to take or give title with.

When buying property, you are referred to as the Grantee and the seller is referred to as the Grantor. (By the way, these then switch and become the exact opposite when you later sell the property, you become the Grantor, and the buyer becomes the Grantee.)

In the sample warranty deed provided, you will replace the numbered items with your own information. This example assumes you are using a Living Trust to hold ownership instead of yourself personally. Get the book entitled "Living Trusts for Real Estate Investors" to learn all the details you need to set up and flip properties inside Living Trusts.

1. Name of the Trust

2. Current Date

3. Name of the Trustee (Grantee)

4. Name of the Seller (Grantor)

5. Address of Trustee (Grantee)

6. Address of Seller (Grantor)

7. N/A

8. The county where the Property is located

9. The state where the Property is located

10. The state where the Notarizing takes place

11. The county where the Notarizing takes place

12. A legal description of a property you wish to buy

WARRANTY DEED

THE STATE OF ___9___ §
                     § KNOW ALL MEN BY THESE PRESENTS:
COUNTY OF ___8___   §

THAT I, ___4___, hereafter referred to as **Grantor**, whose address is _____6_____ whether one or more, for and in consideration of the sum of TEN AND NO/100 ($10.00) DOLLARS and other good and valuable consideration to the undersigned paid by the Grantee herein named, the receipt of which is hereby acknowledged, have GRANTED, SOLD AND CONVEYED, and by these presents do GRANT, SELL AND CONVEY unto the _____1_____, referred to as "**Grantee**," whose address is _____5_____ , all of the following described real property in _____8_____ County, Texas, to-wit:

_____12_____

This conveyance is made subject to any and all reservations of oil, gas and minerals, and valid exceptions, covenants, conditions and restrictions contained in the chain of title of said premises, including sales or reservations of oil, gas and minerals; now of record in the County Clerk's office of _____8_____ County, Texas, but only to the extent they are still in force and effect.

TO HAVE AND TO HOLD the above described premises, together with all and singular the rights and appurtenances thereto in anywise belonging, unto the said grantee, his heirs and assigns forever, and we do hereby bind myself, my heirs, executors and administrators, to WARRANT AND FOREVER DEFEND all and singular the said premises unto the said grantee, his heirs and assigns, against every person whomsoever lawfully claiming or to claim the same or any part thereof.

EXECUTED this _____ day of _____, 20_____

_____4_____ Grantor 1

_____4_____ Grantor 2

THE STATE OF _____10_____   §
                              §
COUNTY OF _____11_____

This instrument was acknowledged before me on this _____ day of _____, 20___ by _____4_____.

_____
Notary Public

| After recording return to: |
| **Place Trustee's Name and Address Here** |

CREATING A SPECIAL WARRANTY DEED

I almost always use a special warranty deed when selling property. If I'm selling through a title company, then I don't create the deed. The title company's lawyer does, and there is usually a title policy in effect, so in those cases, I will use and sign their general warranty deed.

In this section, we will go over how to fill out a special warranty deed when your trust is selling a property or conveying trust property to another person and you are not using a title company or closing attorney.

When selling property, you (trust and trustee) are referred to as the grantor, and the buyer is referred to as the grantee. You will be replacing the following items with your own information.

1. Name of the Trust

2. Current Date

3. Name of the Trustee (Grantor)

4. Name of the Buyer (Grantee)

5. Address of Trustee (Grantor)

6. Address of Buyer (Grantee)

7. N/A

8. The county where the Property is located

9. The state where the Property is located

10. The state where the Notarizing takes place

11. The county where the Notarizing takes place

12. A legal description of a property you wish to buy

SPECIAL WARRANTY DEED

THE STATE OF _____9_____

COUNTY OF _____8_____

§ KNOW ALL MEN BY THESE PRESENTS:

THAT _____3_____, TRUSTEE FOR _____1_____, hereafter referred to as Grantor, whose address is _____5_____, whether one or more, for and in consideration of the sum of TEN AND NO/100 ($10.00) DOLLARS and other good and valuable consideration to the undersigned paid by the Grantee herein named, the receipt of which is hereby acknowledged, have **GRANTED, SOLD AND CONVEYED**, and by these presents do **GRANT, SELL AND CONVEY** unto _____4_____, referred to as "Grantee," whose address is _____6_____, all of the following described real property, to-wit:

_____12_____

This conveyance is made subject to any and all reservations of oil, gas and minerals, and valid exceptions, covenants, conditions and restrictions contained in the chain of title of said premises, including sales or reservations of oil, gas and minerals; now of record in the County Clerk's office of _____8_____, County, Texas, but only to the extent they are still in force and effect.

Grantor binds Grantor and Grantor's heirs, executors, administrators, successors and assigns to warrant and forever defend all and singular the Property to Grantee and Grantee's heirs, executors, administrators, successors, and assigns against every person whomsoever lawfully claiming or to claim the same or any part thereof, when the claim is by, through or under Grantor, but not otherwise, except as to the Reservations from Conveyance and the exceptions to Conveyance and Warranty.

GRANTOR MAKES NO REPRESENTATIONS OR WARRANTIES, EXPRESS OR IMPLIED, AS TO THE SUITABILITY OR FITNESS OF THE PROPERTY FOR ANY PURPOSE, OR AS TO THE VALUE, QUALITY OR CONDITION OF THE PROPERTY. THE SALE OF THE PROPERTY BY GRANTOR TO GRANTEE SHALL BE "AS IS", "WHERE IS", AND "WITH ALL FAULTS." THE FOREGOING PROVISIONS SURVIVE THE DELIVERY OF THIS DEED.

EXECUTED this _____ day of _____, 20_____

_____

_____3_____, TRUSTEE FOR _____1_____,

THE STATE OF _____10_____ §

COUNTY OF _____11_____ §

This instrument was acknowledged before me on this _____ day of _____, 20____ by _____3_____ as Trustee.

_____

Notary Public

My Commission expires: _____

After Recording, Return to:
Name and address of Grantor

HOW TO DO YOUR OWN CHAIN OF TITLE SEARCH

When closing through a title company, they will do the title search and all verifications for you. This section is just for those who are not using a closing agent and doing their own title search on smaller valued properties.

You will want to do a title search of the deed records database in the county where the property is located. The property databases are usually available online if physical access to the county clerk's office is not a convenient drive from your location.

You can also hire it to be done through a title research company such as protitleusa.com (at the time of this writing their cost of a full search was $200) or another similar service. Often, the local county clerk's office can help guide you as to how to search the records in that county.

What you are searching for is a clean title history. Meaning there are no liens against the property and all the prior owners transferred ownership using the proper means and methods as you are learning in this book. For example, a deed that shows a married couple taking ownership at one time but then only one of the couple signed a subsequent deed when they sold it to the next buyer in the chain of title is a problematic issue.

It means only half the property was conveyed, which results in a term we refer to as "bad title." Anything creating a problem issue, most of which we cover here in this section, will create "Bad Title," and must be fixed before taking ownership. If it can't be fixed, then we pass on the deal.

The search is very important if you are not obtaining a title insurance policy. In the beginning, it is best to use a professional search service like protitleusa.com. In time, you may be able to do a better job than the pros.

All real estate investors should know the basics of doing their own title search on properties they are interested in buying. I won't even leave my home to look at a property before I do a quick title search to see who owns it, who they bought it from, and who they bought it from.

Once you learn this information, you should be able to do your own online chain of title search in less than 15 minutes in most cases. You want to see all liens showing they were released and the correct parties passing title along the history of the property. You are looking for any judgments against the current seller or the last seller. You are also looking for any other deeds of trust that may be current against the property.

Once you find any deeds of trust or mortgages without a matching release of lien, then you know that the current owner most likely still has debt owed against the property, and you are in a better position to negotiate with them. Deeds of trust will provide you with the original loan amount and date.

You can estimate the interest rate and plug it into an amortization schedule to get pretty close to their outstanding debt owed on their loan. Another reason I do my own searches is that I buy cheap properties, so cheap in fact, it doesn't always pay me to buy title insurance, so I don't. But I still need to know there aren't any title issues, so I have learned how to do a title search that sometimes outperforms my local title companies.

For example, a while back, I bought a five-acre parcel. The owner had it fall out of closing because they couldn't get the last seller in the chain to give them a release. He was in his 80s and kept telling the title company he already signed off on it years ago, then he would cuss them out and hang up.

Right after the deal fell through, the seller responded to one of my mailings, but they didn't volunteer any of this information. I quickly found the missing release of lien through my own search and confronted the seller with the news. She admitted the real story and then quickly agreed to my low-ball price.

Why did I buy this title problem property? Because while I found that the release was missing and heard the story, it occurred to me to look for the release of lien that the old man insisted he signed, but the title company failed to find. I took every combination of all parties' names I could come up with and did a search on them. Sure enough, there it was - the missing release was filed under another version of their names as husband and wife.

There is no magic computer at a title company doing searches; it's just people. Which means we can learn to do what they do, but we get paid more. And when you can solve title issues (and you will learn how to do this as you do deals), you can buy deals far below their true value.

It is wise to learn more about flipping land inside Living Trusts via my book entitled "Living Trusts for Real Estate Investors." Understanding the title search helps you understand how and why the trust is going to expose names and addresses in the public records, but I expect many of you will be glad to learn this chapter for other reasons as well.

Once you access the database for the county clerk's property search webpage or visit their physical office, search for the current selling party's name(s) by running a search on their individual names. If you don't know the owner's name, look up the county tax records for that address.

Run a search for both names when there are multiple owners or a husband and wife on a property. This is because not all liens or other issues will be found under both parties' names. A wife could have a lien whereas her husband does not. You will run a search on both names individually to find every document filed that concerns that person in the county where the property is located.

When the results come up, search through the list for the property description to find the original conveyance to them. Often a person or couple buys a property, which will create the deed in their personal name(s), and then later, sometimes years later, they convey the property into a family trust.

You can look down the list once you find the property description next to their names, then scan up and down the search results list to see if they show up again as transferring the property into the trust or to other parties. You are also looking for any liens against their name as well.

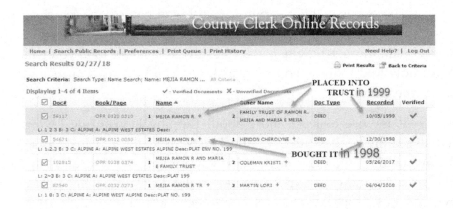

Above, we can see this at work as we did a search for Ramon Mejia (last name first is the norm on county database searches), and any deeds in which he had an ownership interest came up in the search results. We can see that in 1998, he bought the property, which is linked to his deed.

When clicked, it will open and show us a copy of the filed deed itself. He later transferred it to a family trust for him and his wife in 1999. We don't see any tax liens, garnishments, or other issues filed against his name.

We will grab both of these deeds and make sure the legal and listed names on the deed all match, so we have a valid transfer from him to the trust. Then we will do the same thing with his wife Maria E Mejia. (I suggest doing searches with and without the middle initials).

The same deed and trust will come up again, but we are also looking down the list to see if any liens or deeds of trust are showing in her name as well. If you do find one, then open that document and try to figure out if they are referring to the same person and if it is something that is attached to this property.

This can often be figured out by looking at the addresses on the documents and the dates of similar active time frames that seem logical. The final way to figure it out is to ask the person if they are the same person as the person with the lien or other claim against them.

How Liens Attach and Follow a Property

Liens filed against a person after they conveyed a property into a trust do not attach to that property. However, if an owner transferred their property after a lien has been filed in the deed of records, then it attaches and it stays attached until it is either paid off, negotiated off, or falls off under the Statutes of Limitations for that type of lien in that state.

Using Mrs. Mejia above as an example, if a tax lien had been filed against her a month before she and her husband transferred the property into the trust, it would mean the lien attached to the property. The lien attached to it and stays with the property even though they conveyed it into a trust.

But, if you found that they deeded the property into the trust even a day before a lien was filed against her, then the property is free of the lien, as the lien only affects property she would have personally owned in her name on the date of the filing of the lien.

Here is some interesting insight: even though a judgment doesn't attach to property held in a trust prior to the judgment being filed, the judgment holder could petition the court to pull the property out of the trust and convey it to the judgment holder if they were aware the defendant was the trustor of a trust holding assets.

But it is not often done because the holders and their lawyers don't see any connection in public records between the person they sued and the trust they control holding assets, not if they did it right. They don't bother questioning the defendant with interrogatories and other discovery methods as to their possible position as trustor or trustee since that is an extra expense to the plaintiff. This is a classic example of why you want to use trusts; it layers protection for you.

This is what you are always looking for: situations where liens attach or people haven't conveyed properly. In this case, we see she is just fine, no liens have ever been filed against her, so we then move on to the next grantor in the chain of title.

Similar Name Lien Issues

Similar names will often come up in your searches. If a name doesn't have a middle initial listed in the search results, you will need to open each lien document you see, as that name could be your seller's name.

Once you look at the document, it may prove not to be the same person, but if you are in doubt, just ask the seller if that is their lien. If not, you can ask them to provide you an affidavit stating they are not the same person as the person listed with the lien.

I've seen liens against the son of a seller whose name is the same as the father's, but they left off the "Jr." In cases like that, you will have to ask the seller to determine the results.

Dates of when it happened help clue you in, as well as the addresses of those parties found on any filed document during the time frame as the lien. Also, remember, it is for the most part, only an issue with liens listed in the last ten years. Unreleased deeds of trusts or mortgages can attach to the title much longer; they could affect the title for many decades.

Deed of Trust Liens

In your search of the subject property in the deed of records, whenever you find a warranty deed filed under the owner's name, look next to this document in the nearby time frame and see if there was a deed of trust also filed in the seller's name; often on the same day as the deed was filed.

A deed of trust is a lien against the property; it means there was a loan taken out when the warranty deed was created and the warranty deed is now subject to this deed of trust lien until the loan is paid back. In many states, they will title this warranty deed "General Warranty Deed with Vendor's Lien" so you know that a deed of trust was filed as well.

Once the loan is paid off, the lender will file a document called a "Release of Lien" which removes the lien. Therefore, you will want to look for a release of lien for every deed of trust you find listed against a seller.

You can look down the search results to locate the release. It often might be many years later before you find the release since it can take a while to either pay off the loan or resell the property.

Expect to find a release of lien sometime after it was last sold in the search results. If you don't find one, it means they may still have some outstanding balance owed which needs to be paid off at closing in most cases.

Other times, you may find a deed of trust with no release of lien filed even though the seller claims it was paid off. This is likely because the lender forgot to file it. In that case, ask the seller to find the lender and request they file it; otherwise, it has "bad title" and you shouldn't close on the property.

Sometimes, banks go under or get closed by the government. If they do, they or the government will sell off the lender's loans to other banks or lenders. There may be an indication of that in the filings where one bank assigned a deed of trust to another bank called an "Assignment of Deed of Trust" (AKA "Assignment of Trust Deed" or "Assignment of Mortgage"). If not, Google search the bank or mortgage company to find out who the loans were transferred to. This will be rare, but I've had to do it a couple of times.

After establishing the names of the parties in the initial index search of the deed of records or utilizing an outside service, continue doing a chain of title search going back at least 30 years or until the subdivision the property is located in was created.

You are going to daisy-chain search the deeds back in history to make sure no outstanding liens were placed against the property that haven't expired or been released, including deeds of trust, mortgages, IRS tax liens, state liens, or judgments. Any of these items showing up in the chain of title history can present a problem that needs addressing before closing.

Missing Names of Sellers in the Clerk's Records

If the names of the sellers you are dealing with don't appear in the search, it is often because they inherited the property and it was never conveyed to them by deed. While they are the rightful heirs and could have been paying taxes for years on the property, nobody transferred the title into their name, or they never filed it.

In that case, they don't have clean title to the property and they can't convey title to you since it is not in their name(s). In rare cases, the seller may have an unrecorded deed and you can simply file that one to cure the problem.

If the issue is one of inheritance in which no Last Will and Testament was probated, then you can often fix this situation for them by helping them obtain a blank "Affidavit of Heirship" form they can fill out and notarize.

You will then file the notarized affidavit at the same time you file the deed. This will pass good title to your trust.

An affidavit of heirship must show their (the sellers') names, or their names along with their siblings' names, as the only heirs to the last owners of record.

If they have siblings, you will have each sibling provide you with a notarized special warranty deed. You will then file the affidavit of heirship and the various deeds that they provided you with the County Clerk's Deed of Records Office for the county of where that property is located.

You may have to research the laws of inherited property in your state to learn how to do this. For the first few, you may want to have a local attorney do the affidavit for you. Expect to pay $500 to $1000 for that service. Ask a local real estate attorney how many people need to sign the affidavit of heirship and who is allowed to sign it, or Google the information for your state.

Often, states will allow one of the sellers who may benefit from the sale to sign and two other affidavits must come from people who have no interest in the property. Google your state's affidavit of heirship requirements for more information.

This is another reason people like dealing with someone who understands how these things can be fixed without bringing in a lawyer. It is all available on the internet when you are ready to learn how the affidavit of heirship works in your state and what the requirements are for filling one out. There are boilerplate forms for affidavits of heirship online.

Continuing with the daisy chain search, let's assume you find their name, just as we did with Ramon Mejia above, we saw a listing in the search that showed us he bought the property in 1998 from a party listed as Hendon, Cherolyne (a grantor).

You will then put Hendon, Cherolyne into the search bar and see who they bought it from and if they had any open liens during their ownership, just as we did for the Mejias'. Then keep tracing back grantors' names until you have gone back to the creation of the subdivision or at least 30 years.

Remember, each time you find a couple owning the property, you will need to do a single search on the other name as well, to make sure no liens etc., show up that are still active.

Once you complete the daisy chain search, you should be good to proceed with the transaction. My personal rule is simple: if I'm dealing with land where the value is less than $10,000, then I'm alright with accepting my own search as good enough and will proceed to closing with only my search.

If I'm dealing with a lot over $10,000, while I will proceed to closing, it would be better for my buyer to get a title search done by a professional title company or real estate attorney, but that's still not my call; it's the buyer's decision to make.

Why under $10,000? Because I will have less than $10,000 invested and that amount is not worth having to pay upwards of $500 or more for title insurance, which will equal out to ten thousand in closing costs with a title company/closing attorney over twenty deals.

I'm not going to have a title problem every twenty deals; therefore, it is better to "self-insure" on land lot deals or even small home deals (rehabs) below the 10k level. Besides, if I missed something and am challenged, the value of the property will not be worth the plaintiff paying out $5,000 in legal fees to get back a $10,000 property.

And at most, we can negotiate a much smaller payoff than the $10,000, and I'm still ahead financially even if I lose. A challenge is very uncommon, and it has not happened to me yet. That's also because if I see any issues that don't look simple enough to fix, I will pass on that transaction. Don't buy a porcupine of a property; pass it up and buy the next one. There are plenty of properties that have clean title histories, especially in the land area.

Most lot properties I buy never even had a lien on them, so you will often find a series of clean warranty or special warranty deeds down through the chain of title and very often only one or two owners appear in the chain of title.

Red flags arise when you see bankruptcy, tax liens, etc. In those cases, you want to be safe and obtain title insurance or pass on them.

If you come up with an issue in the chain of title, don't just stop at the first signs of a problem; look up the situation online. An internet search will give you a lot of answers on how to fix many title issues, such as affidavits of heirship, judgments, tax liens, etc.

Most can be fixed by researching how others online or in forums fix them and by understanding what your state statutes say about the issue. Always verify you are dealing with your property's state laws in which it is located, and not a different state when looking up solutions online. If someone is discussing liens, then it must be according to the proper state. Online lawyers can be a big help as well for a small fee and emailed answers.

Becoming adept at looking up your own state statutes that discuss what you are researching is crucial in becoming an expert in fixing property issues. As you gain experience, you may find yourself creating niches by targeting properties with specific problems that you know how to resolve, allowing you to purchase them at a significant discount and turn them into profitable deals.

Mastering the techniques for searching and dealing with title issues can take a year or more, but you don't have to know everything to start doing your own searches. In the meantime, you can always rely on professional services to handle your title searches, and title insurance is available as an added layer of protection.

The basics provided here on searching the title history of properties are intended to help you protect yourself and your investment. Remember that learning this art is an ongoing process, so don't feel like you need to know everything before you begin conducting your own searches.

Conducting your own searches primarily serves to help you determine if you should continue pursuing a deal and to avoid wasting time on properties with title problems or on smaller deals where purchasing title insurance may not be cost-effective. However, if you choose to do your own searches, you must be prepared to accept the risks associated with potentially missing certain issues. This is all part of risk management in the world of real estate investing.

Finishing up the Deed after the Search

Now that you have completed the title search and found no issues, you can proceed with preparing the deed to transfer the title from the Mejias' trust to your trust. To do this, you'll need to gather the key information from the previous two deeds (the deed transferring to their personal name and the later deed transferring to their trust). This information includes the grantee names and the legal description of the property. You can copy the name of the trust and trustee directly from the existing deed onto your new deed.

QUITCLAIM DEED

THE FOLLOWING GRANTOR(S):	Ramon R. Mejia and Maria E. Mejia
NAME OF TRUSTEE(S):	Ramon R. Mejia and Maria E. Mejia
NAME OF TRUST:	Family Trust of Ramon R. Mejia and Maria E. Mejia
DATE OF TRUST DOCUMENT:	June 24, 1999
CITY OF:	Alpine
COUNTY OF:	Brewster
STATE OF:	Texas
SAID REAL PROPERTY IS DESCRIBED AS FOLLOWS:	All of Lots One (1), Two (2), and Three (3), Block Three (3), Alpine West Estates, Alpine, Brewster County, Texas, as the same appears in Plat Envelope No. 199 on file in the office of the County Clerk of Brewster County, Texas.
Date:	June 24, 1999

The above ownership transfer was done with a quitclaim deed, unusual, but still legal and common. It could have also been completed using a warranty deed, a grant deed, or even a special warranty deed with the same information.

I imposed arrows on the document above to show you the information we need in order to fill out our warranty deed from the trustees online information.

The various names can be transferred to the default deeds I provide you with in this book. Just fill them in from the information taken from the previous deed like the above quitclaim deed, and use the legal description from the prior deed as well. It is that easy to take ownership from the trust. Here is what that will look like:

> THAT I, **Ramon R. Mejia and Maria E. Mejia, Trustees for the Family Trust of Ramon R. Mejia and Maria E. Mejia**, hereafter referred to as Grantor, whose address is 444 Main St, Grady, TX 76642, whether one or more, for and in consideration of the sum of TEN AND NO/100 ($10.00) DOLLARS and other good and valuable consideration to the undersigned paid by the Grantee herein named, the receipt of which is hereby acknowledged, have GRANTED, SOLD AND CONVEYED, and by these presents do GRANT, SELL AND CONVEY unto the **Dallas 5883 TRUST**, referred to as "**Grantee**," whose address is 63 Woodberry, Dallas, State of Texas, all of the following described real property in **Dallas** County, Texas, to-wit

To create your new deed, transfer the relevant information from the existing quitclaim deed to the default deeds provided in your materials. This will include the names of the trustees and the trust, their address, and the legal description of the property. Once you've filled in this information, the deed will have signature lines for both trustees at the bottom. The trustees will sign the deed in front of a notary public, and once that is done, the deed is ready to be filed at the deed of records office.

With the deed prepared and signed, you can proceed with filing it to officially transfer ownership of the property to your trust.

How to Correct Legal Documents Before and After Filing

Yes, it is possible to correct mistakes on legal documents like deeds or deeds of trust before filing them. Unlike sales contracts, where both parties need to initial any changes for them to be legal, deeds can be amended without requiring the other party's initials. However, it is crucial to review your deed carefully before filing or mailing it to minimize the chances of errors.

If you have already filed a deed and later realize there is a mistake, you will need to refile the deed with a corrected version of the document. While the procedure for correcting filed documents may vary slightly from state to state, the general process is as follows:

1. Using a copy of the filed document, type in the correct information to make the necessary correction in the text.
2. Add the word "Corrected" to the title of the document. For example, "General Warranty Deed" becomes "Corrected Warranty Deed."
3. Just below the title of the document, briefly explain the change made in the document. This should include reference to the date and filing number stamped on the originally filed document by the county. For example:

Corrected Special Warranty Deed

This corrects a deed filed on 4-3-2018 (Document #20185539) in which the legal description contained a mistake as to the Lot number.

---

4. Have the signing party notarize the corrected document.
5. File the corrected document with the county clerk.

Before using the information above, be sure to verify the procedure for correcting filed documents in your state, as some states may have additional steps or requirements.

How to Utilize Mobile Notaries

Your process for buying property from out-of-town or out-of-state sellers is a viable approach for handling remote closings. Using a mobile notary to facilitate the closing process is a practical solution that ensures the necessary documents are signed and notarized, and the sellers receive their payment.

Here's a summary of your process:

1. Contract to buy the property using a purchase agreement.
2. When ready to close, draw up the deed yourself.
3. Send the deed, cashier's check, and a simple closing statement to a mobile notary.
4. Instruct the notary to have the sellers sign the deed and a copy of the closing statement.
5. The notary public gives the check to the sellers.
6. The notary public overnights the signed and notarized deed and a copy of the closing statement back to you.
7. File the deed with the county.

Most mobile notaries charge a reasonable fee for their services, and they are bonded, which means you can trust them with your cashier's check. It's always a good idea to verify the active status of a mobile notary by looking them up on their state website of licensed notaries.

Overall, your process is efficient and enables you to conduct real estate transactions with sellers who live far away from your location.

Most notaries will charge you $30-$125 for this service. Larger cities like Los Angeles, New York City, and Chicago may cost a little more. I usually pay the notary with a money order in the same package, but you can arrange payment with them according to their customary practices.

DINING-ROOM TABLE CLOSING

This section will not dwell on formal title or attorney closings, as they are done for you; you simply show up, sign a bunch of documents, pick up the check, and you are done. Now, we will look at self-closing your own transactions.

I self-close most of my transactions. It saves me tens of thousands every year. Moreover, it is far more enjoyable and much faster to close your own smaller deals than having a title company do it for you. You should be able to self-close your smaller deals in a couple of days at most, compared to a few weeks to a month with a title closing company.

The term "dining-room closing" has been used for many years in investor circles to indicate the closing of a transaction that does not involve a title company or closing attorney. The closing often happens at the subject property or at the seller's or buyer's dining-room table.

Each side closes with you individually without the other side being present. This means that you and the seller meet and hold that closing. Then, at another closing, often days later, you and the buyer meet to hold that closing.

You, as the investor, usually supply all the documents, while the buyer brings the funds to close the deal. The closing is simply getting everyone's signatures on the right documents.

You can hire a mobile notary to notarize the deeds and trust deeds, or you can drive to a notary's office and close in their waiting room.

The notary is not a lawyer and will not get into your transactions with questions, etc.; they only verify signatures on documents. This means you control the closing, not the notary.

The dining-room closing is really a self-closing transaction, and I will use that term going forward. I will go over the process I have used for many years to close my own deals without a title company or attorney since it is a time-tested and practical way to self-close.

This is not to say you shouldn't use a title company on larger deals; as I have cautioned, I only do this with transactions under $10,000, mainly small land or lot deals or teardown houses that have land value only.

A self-closing transaction involves completing the transaction with the seller or the buyer, providing each party with copies of all the documents, and either paying or getting paid at that closing. Federal law requires that all real estate closings utilize a formal Closing Statement, which is a document that shows the financial details of the transaction, the names of the parties, and the property purchased or sold.

The closing statement will list closing costs as well. It should always show clearly how much was paid at closing from one party to the other party and account for all the money paid by a buyer to a seller. I use a very simple form to complete this requirement. These documents are mainly for use with each party's tax returns and for proving details of the closing to each party. (See an example of a closing statement at the end of this section.)

How to Self-close with Sellers

First, I have discussed briefly elsewhere in the book how I buy from sellers, but I will cover more detail here on how I buy from out-of-town or out-of-state sellers, as they are my most common type of seller and could be your most common type of seller once you know how to close with them.

If I'm using a title company or closing attorney, then the agent will usually FedEx the closing package to the seller, and they sign the documents in front of a notary and mail them back. Some agents will mail the package directly to a mobile notary and have them handle the closing. If the title company has a branch office in the same city, they may mail the package to that office and have them handle the signing. Once the seller signs off, then my local office will call me, and I will go in or my trustee will go in and sign the documents to finish.

If I'm not using a closing agent, then I do a self-closing via FedEx with the seller. I mail them a closing package when I'm ready to pay them. The package is overnighted to a mobile notary who acts as my agent in the closing.

Notaries are bonded and do these kinds of closings for title companies all the time, so I feel safe trusting them with my cashier's checks that get handed to the sellers. I find the notaries on a website called 123notary.com and have used them for many years without a single problem worth talking about.

I begin the closing process with a seller by calling them once I'm ready to pay for the property. I inform them I'll be contacting a local notary in their city or nearby to handle the closing. The notary can meet them at the seller's bank, where the notary will hand them my cashier's check and have them sign a closing statement and a deed.

Once I explain the process to the seller, I go online and find a local mobile notary by searching with the seller's zip code at 123notary.com and call a notary as close as possible to the seller. Once I find one that can work with the date and time the seller provided me, I get the cost, their mailing address, and let them know to expect an overnight FedEx from me.

I give them the address of the local bank where they are to meet the seller. I then create a package with two copies of everything, namely the deed, the closing statement, and any other document that might have to be signed, like an affidavit of heirship, for example.

I will also print out a Notary Instruction Page containing the seller's contact information, where and when to meet, and what to get signed and sent back to me. I will also place into the package the return FedEx label and put it in an empty return FedEx envelope so the notary can drop the envelope in a local drop box, sending the package back to me. This gets the deed back to me overnight as well.

A few times, I've had the notary meet the seller at the seller's home when the seller can't leave for various reasons. But most of the time, the meeting place is the seller's bank, as they know it is safe, and they can deposit my check right away.

If the seller lives close to me, I might meet them myself, but I find even driving more than 20 minutes away costs me more in time and gas than the cost of a mobile notary.

How to Self-Close with Buyers

As for buyers, I will create the deed and a closing statement for them as well. If they are local, I will usually have them meet me at the county clerk's office where they deliver their funds to me, and together, we file the deed at the Clerk's office. It helps them feel safe knowing that their deed is filed at the time they pay for the property.

They will normally pay me with a cashier's check, and I will file the deed and have the clerk make them a copy they can take home that day. Their address is also in the "return after filing" box on the deed, so they get sent the original deed in a few weeks. I have them sign a copy of the closing statement, and the deal is completed.

Never file a deed before you have good funds in your hands, meaning a cashier's check or, at worst, money orders. Don't ever take a personal check. You can't un-file a deed once it is filed with the county when you find out you were given a hot check or received a charge-back from a credit card service. It takes a civil action to get your property back in those cases, so always make sure you have good funds before filing the deed. The second you file the deed, ownership has passed, and it can't be undone.

It is a very fast process. Once we meet, I show them the deed and verify all their information (name and address) is correct. I then show them the closing statement and go over it. I will take their check at that point and write down the check number and the bank it was drawn on for tax purposes. I then give them a copy of the closing statement, and we walk into the clerk's office and file the deed.

I will have the clerk make a copy of the filed deed at that time and hand it to the buyer in the clerk's office. The whole thing takes about 10 minutes to complete unless you like conversations, which I do. I use the same basic closing statement for both sellers and buyers; the only things that change are the names, sales number, and legal address of the property.

Closing Statement

Sale Closed March 16, 2018

Buyer: **Carol Brady**

Address: 612 Edward Ln. Irving, TX 78555

Seller: **Jay Smith, Trustee of the Bally Trust,**

Address: 55 Main St, Dallas TX 75882

Property Legal Address:

Lot 3, in Block 5, Section 6, in Knee-Bend Subdivision, Dallas County Texas

---

Sales Price: $14,000.00

Earnest money previously paid: $5,000.00

Closing Costs paid by Buyer $300.00

Balance paid today to seller: $9,300.00 paid by Cashier's Check number #4455998694 drawn on XYZ Bank

Signatures:

Seller: _____ as trustee

Buyer: _____

HOW JUDGMENTS AND LIENS CAN BE OVERCOME

When someone claims another person owes them money, they can take the debtor to court, obtain a judgment against them, and then file an "Abstract of Judgment" with the county clerk in the county where the debtor owns or may own property in the future. Once this judgment is filed, it acts as a lien against any property currently owned by the debtor or might own in the future, as long as the judgment is active.

The way a lien is removed is by the debtor coming to terms with the judgment holder for what is owed, and then the judgment holder files a formal document with the county clerk called a "Release of Lien." This is similar to the way a deed of trust is removed from a property when payments have finished being made to the holder of the deed of trust. Once the debtor pays off the lender, the lender will file a release of lien.

A common problem arises when debtors settle these issues, but the holder of the debt fails to file the release, thus leaving a lien in place and preventing the owner from selling their property with a good title. The cure to this is to have the seller call the lender and mail a formal letter requesting they file a release of lien. If they fail to file the release of lien document with the deed of records, they could be subject to a court order.

The real issue arises when the debtor didn't pay off their debt. In these cases, you might still be able to handle these cases and find yourself a great deal because a lien is still attached to the property.

Most liens have a time limitation, which can be found by looking up your state's "statute of limitations." After identifying the type of lien, such as an IRS tax lien or mechanic's lien, determine how long that type of lien remains active once it is filed. Look up the process for extending them in your state as well, so you understand that process too.

For example, in most states, judgments that have been filed in the deed of records will only remain valid for 10 years and then become void by default. If the abstract of judgment is not refiled into the deed of records in a short window before the tenth year, the judgment can be ignored in your search for liens.

However, if you see the lien has been refiled into the deed of records, that lien will stay active for another 10 years. It is rare to see a lien being extended, but IRS liens have been known to be extended in the 9th year, and some have expired as they were not extended.

Hospital liens are very common, and they almost always expire without being extended by the judgment holder. They, like all other liens, can also be "negotiated" away. Additionally, most sellers don't realize that judgments drop off after ten years, so they are negotiating from a lack of understanding of the law.

Offer to Buy the Lien at a Discount

Just because you find a lien, it doesn't mean you can't fix the situation. The party that filed it may be willing to accept a small fraction of the original amount to release it. One way to do this is to offer to buy the judgment. Write the lien holder and offer them a low-ball amount to purchase the lien.

Most have already written off the possibility of ever being paid anything, so they may accept next to nothing as an offer. If they refuse your offer, they know they most likely will never get another offer, and that makes your offer hard to turn down.

There are businesses nationwide that buy these judgments, and they often offer the same pennies on the dollar offers. This means you could be a similar type of buyer of judgments, but in this case, you are only after this one, at a greatly reduced price.

Your state statutes will inform you about time limits on liens (search the term "Statute of Limitation Credit Card Lien Ohio" or whatever lien you want to learn about) in the state where the property is located. Most of this kind of information is available on the internet, including full state statutes and even lawyers giving online advice about similar questions.

Liens that Don't Expire

Liens that don't expire are state and county tax liens. They remain in effect until the taxes owed on the lien are paid. After those are paid, along with interest, any taxes that continued to accrue will also still be owed, even though they are not part of the lien.

If this kind of lien is filed, then find out how much tax is owed by calling the state or county tax department and asking for both the payoff amount as well as the penalties and interests that are accruing outside the lien, which would have continued to be owed yearly. If it is still a good deal, you will know it and can buy the property and pay off the taxes at closing.

You Can Always Pay the Lien Off at Closing The last avenue for dealing with a lien is to tell the seller that they can use your funds at closing to pay it off or go toward paying it off. They may accept that they have to pay it off, as there is no other choice. Otherwise, you will know to pass on the purchase of this property.

Here is what a state or county judgment might look like.

ABSTRACT OF JUDGMENT
40-01-168

40157

REQ: 8 20 93

REAL PROPERTY RECORDS

THE STATE OF TEXAS
COUNTY OF TRAVIS

NAME:

FILED:

I, Jade Meeker, Justice of the Peace Pct. No. 5 of Travis County, Texas do hereby certify that in the Justice of the Peace Pct. No. 5 Court of Travis County, Texas, in a certain suit pending in said Court, Cause No. 156,849, wherein THE STATE OF TEXAS, plaintiff, and A⸺ ⸺ T SMITH RE: ⸺⸺ S SMITH defendant, WHOSE SOCIAL SECURITY NUMBER IS: C 4⸺ 21 46⸺ 2C, whose birthdate and drivers license number is not available to the clerk, who was served with citation at: ⸺ 112 PARK MANOR, ⸺ ⸺, TX 7⸺ ⸺-5⸺6 the said plaintiff, THE STATE OF TEXAS recovered judgment against said defendant ⸺ ⸺⸺ T SMITH RE: ⸺⸺⸺ S SMITH on the 23rd day of MARCH, 1993; for the sum of $3,053.11; THREE THOUSAND FIFTY-THREE AND .11 DOLLARS, with interest on said amount from the 23rd day of MARCH, 1993, At the rate per annum as listed hereinafter:

734.00   .1000
734.00   .1000
450.00   .1000
450.00   .1000

and $45.00 costs of suit.

Said judgment is entitled to the following credits, to-wit: 0.00. There are still due on said judgment the amounts as hereinabove set out, with interest on said amounts as hereinabove set out, and $45.00 cost of suit.

Given under my hand of office at Austin, Texas this ⸺⸺ day of **SEP 2 1 1993**, 19⸺

Jade Meeker, Justice of the Peace, Pct. No. 5
Travis County, Texas

STATE OF TEXAS
I hereby certify that this instrument was filed in File Number Sequence on the date and at the time stamped herein by me and was duly RECORDED in the official Public Records of Real Property of Montgomery County, Texas.

Return to:
Texas Higher Education
Coordinating Board
P O Box 12788
Austin, Tx 78711

JAN - 7 1994

Roy H ⸺
COUNTY CLERK

In the above example, the text mentions that the plaintiff is "The State of Texas"; otherwise, it might mention something in regards to delinquent taxes and that the plaintiff is the county or state. As such, we know this is one of those judgments that doesn't have a time limitation. It also states the balance will continue to grow due to penalties and interest. Understand that taxes will continue to come due and become delinquent from the date of the judgment. This is what makes property tax liens difficult to deal with. Often, they become higher than the value of the property, especially in land/lot deals.

You might normally pass on these since you don't want to invest the time to find out. However, this means investors who have more time than money can pick up this type of deal at a bargain price. The more you learn how to deal with problem title issues, the more money you can make.

Bankruptcy Issues

If the seller or any company they own is going through a current bankruptcy proceeding, then you would need to obtain permission from the court-appointed Receiver before closing on any property connected to that person/company.

The bankruptcy court is very powerful and can reach very far to pull property into a bankruptcy. People often try to hide property in trusts and corporate entities. You can never assume the property of someone in an active bankruptcy is free of the court's reach.

This means that if a seller puts property into some entity, then later goes into bankruptcy and tries to sell it to you, you will always want to ask the court or the receiver if it is acceptable for you to purchase that property.

A bankruptcy judge can reach into various entities holding property where an illegal transfer occurred and take that property away from the new owner, placing it into the bankruptcy proceedings.

If you bought it from a person in the middle of a bankruptcy, you could stand to lose the money you paid and the property.

It is always a good idea to run a bankruptcy search on a seller before buying from them. You can run a nationwide search by getting a free Pacer Account at (**https://pcl.uscourts.gov**).

Run a search on the names of any party claiming ownership listed on the deed. If they are not listed on the deed and a trust is the only listed party, then ask to see the trust document or certification of trust to determine who the trustor is and run the search on the trustor. This applies to corporations and limited liability companies as well.

How to Double Close in a Title or Lawyer Office

The double close is one of the most common flipping strategies used today and is a favorite among many investors. It gives you more control within the transaction, as you do own the property, even if only for a few minutes or a day. Additionally, it allows you to avoid many of the new laws on wholesaling that states are now passing, which makes it more challenging to wholesale flip.

In a double closing flip, you will contract to buy a property and use the money from the buyer at closing to buy from the seller. (Side note): If your seller breaches the contract, you can file a "Memorandum of Contract" to lock in your position with the seller at the deed of records office.

Under the new privacy laws, title companies can split the Closing Documents up so the Seller and the Buyer never see each other's side of the transaction where you are making your profit spread. However, most of these land deals don't go through a title company; instead, you can carry out the double close yourself, as detailed in this book.

BONUS SECTION

Here is a secret gem known as eBay. This site is a great way to find deeply discounted deals if you know what to look for and how to do some basic research on the property before you buy it.

We will examine each of these aspects along with understanding the legal documents involved for those wanting to truly understand the correct process for buying land from anyone, anywhere, including eBay.

Many people like to buy land for a future home site, as an investment, or just to collect land since they are not making any more of it. If you are buying for current or future use, then you should learn the tools and process of buying land as detailed within this book.

It is almost a given that when you buy land on eBay, you probably already know that you can always relist it back up for sale yourself on eBay and most likely get back what you paid for it.

As years go by, you can expect to get even more than you paid for it. Of course, there are no guarantees that would happen, but in my over 30 years of buying and selling land, I found it most often goes up over time.

I've even reposted land for sale and found I got more for it one week than I did before; you just never know who is currently looking to buy and at what price.

Sure, you never know exactly what it will bring, but as for buying it, I do know that eBay is your best friend when it comes to buying dirt cheap land (pun intended).

To give you an idea of how cheaply you can find land on eBay, on a poorly written ad for a parcel, with limited information, and assuming it is being offered in a "no reserve", "high bid wins" style auction, you can often win that parcel for about 10% of its true value.

I have found that for my land that I have sold on eBay with well-documented ads and all the key information available for the buyer to research themselves, the land will bring a final auction price of about 25% to 30% of its cash value when sold in a "no reserve, no minimum, high bid wins" style auction.

By the way, that style auction is the best method for finding the lowest-priced land available. The other ways eBay sellers sell land is by offering it at a "Buy Now" price, which is a price they set, usually 50% to 80% of the true appraised value. Or they offer it for sale by having the bidding for the "Down payment" amount, then the final price is again, a fixed price the seller decides on beforehand.

I'm not saying they don't also offer great deals here and there using those types of auctions, but nothing beats the auction-only style where the beginning bid is often just $1.00, or even $100 to $300. This means that even if the bid goes no further than that, it will be sold.

I've seen some property sell for under $100.00 that should have gone for $2,000.00 just because the descriptions were lacking or the lot truly was not a very good lot. Still, land in the worst condition or location is always worth something, often $1,000 or more. Conversely, you can find land you can buy for $3,000 that could be worth $30,000 (more or less).

So now let's look at some ways we can use this information to flip lots on eBay.

Once you have a little money saved up, maybe from my self-funding method, you might want to start looking for super cheap lots as I detailed above.

Buy and close on it with the eBay seller; next, you list that property in the Facebook Marketplace, rather than going right back onto eBay. You can expect to get a much higher price by selling lots on Facebook to retail buyers in the local area where the lot is situated.

You can also offer owner financing to buyers and further raise the price even higher than selling at a cash price.

By following the strategies outlined in this book and using platforms like eBay and Facebook Marketplace, you can leverage your knowledge and resources to find and flip land at a profit. The key is to do your research, understand the legal documents involved, and be patient as you navigate the land-buying process.

As you gain experience and develop a keen eye for great deals, you will be better equipped to identify opportunities for profit. With time and persistence, you can build a successful land investment portfolio and create a sustainable source of income through land flipping.

Summary

This book provides an in-depth guide to flipping properties, specifically focusing on land deals, and presents valuable information and strategies that can help anyone looking to enter the real estate investment world. The guide covers various aspects of flipping, from understanding the basics of land deals to mastering advanced techniques such as the double close. It equips the reader with the necessary tools and knowledge to successfully navigate the ever-evolving landscape of real estate investment.

One of the most critical aspects of flipping properties is finding the right deals. The book details how to source potential investments, emphasizing the importance of research and due diligence. It highlights the role of public records and online resources, such as county websites, in finding information about properties and their owners. Additionally, it discusses the value of building relationships with professionals, such as real estate agents, attorneys, and title companies, who can provide insights and help facilitate transactions.

The guide also delves into the process of acquiring properties, explaining the various types of contracts and agreements involved. It covers how to negotiate terms with sellers, as well as the importance of a thorough title search to ensure a clear title. The book outlines the steps for preparing and filing deeds, highlighting the significance of accurate information and the potential risks associated with accepting personal checks or other unreliable forms of payment.

One of the primary focuses of the book is the double close strategy, which is a favorite among many investors. This method allows the investor to own the property for a short period, using the funds from the buyer at closing to pay the seller. The double close offers more control within the transaction and helps investors avoid the new laws on wholesaling that can make flipping more challenging. The book provides a detailed explanation of how to execute this strategy and the legal considerations to keep in mind, such as filing a Memorandum of Contract in case the seller breaches the agreement.

In addition to the double close, the book explores other flipping strategies and their respective advantages and challenges. It discusses the benefits of acquiring properties with liens, as well as the process of negotiating with lienholders to release the liens at a fraction of the amount owed. The guide also addresses the issue of sellers involved in bankruptcy proceedings, emphasizing the need to obtain permission from the court-appointed Receiver before closing on any property connected to the person or company in bankruptcy.

Throughout the book, the importance of understanding state laws and regulations is emphasized. It highlights the need to research state-specific statutes of limitations for different types of liens and explains how to access this information online. Moreover, the guide underscores the significance of being aware of privacy laws that affect title companies and the disclosure of transaction details.

The book not only provides a comprehensive overview of flipping properties but also instills a sense of confidence in the reader by sharing practical tips and real-life examples. It empowers investors to tackle complex transactions, such as those involving liens or bankruptcies, by equipping them with the knowledge and skills to navigate these situations successfully. By following the guidance provided in this book, both novice and experienced investors can take advantage of the lucrative opportunities in the world of real estate investment and achieve their financial goals through flipping properties.

BOOKS BY JOHN ALEXANDER

Available at https://JohnAlexander.com

Living Trusts for Real Estate Investors

Stop Exposing Your Name and Assets to Lawsuits and Competition

Corporate entities have their place as liability protection, but they don't protect all the other properties the company may own, and they certainly don't hide what you own and where your properties are located.

It also informs your competition exactly what you are doing, and in what part of the city you found your sweet-spot for great real estate to flip. And if you hold real estate as a long-term investment, as in rentals, you want even more privacy.

You will also learn:
How to conduct your own title searches
How to self-close your own transactions
How to create your own deeds and closing documents
How to file them yourself.

Who Needs This Book?
Wholesalers
Double Closers
Land Flippers
Landlords-Owners

Don't make the mistakes I did when I started advertising land on Facebook!...

I wasted a ton of ad dollars until I figured it out!...

A simple and affordable way to make Facebook algorithms work for you!...

Learn the secrets of creating the perfect land ad for Facebook Marketplace! I list all my land flips on Facebook Marketplace and in this book, I'll show you exactly how we do it to get our land sold fast and at top price.

From crafting the right title and category to properly organizing photos, boosting visibility, and ensuring compliance with Facebook's housing regulations.

"How to Discount Notes"
How to buy Discounted Notes and how to Flip Discounted Notes. This is a complete course on how to run your own Discounted Note Brokering or Investing business.
You will learn every aspect of being a Discounted Note Broker in these pages, from my proven ways of finding unlimited notes -to using my mortgage purchase agreement (included) to locking in the flip to my list of favorite note wholesale buyers. They will buy almost any kind of payment stream, even newly created notes.

You will even learn how to buy and flip notes on auction sites. Single or bulk note purchases from small banks, to finding notes from online county deed records, it's all here, everything I've learned over 35 years in the note business.

This book is a course I sold for many years at prices from $300 to over $1000 in various seminar formats.

I have now made the information available in book form that anyone can afford. I keep it up to date so you know the methods in the latest edition is what is working right now in the discounted note industry.

This book is considered the Note Broker's Bible in the Discount Note Brokering and Note Investing industry for many years.

You will learn how to buy a full note, a partial note, partial payments, full balloon note, part of a balloon note, part of the monthly payment and part of any balloon. All done with both financial calculators and John's free online note broking calculators that make it super easy to create different offers depending on what the note holder needs.

New for 2018 is how the Dodd-Frank Act affects the note business and I reveal my favorite type of note to create, hold, and flip that doesn't fall under the Dodd-Frank regulations. Yet, it is one of the safest notes available today.

This note can be flipped to private investor or even Self-Directed IRA holders paying out a yield up to 20%.

I also share my top method for creating 20% to 30% yielding notes that you can keep or flip to investors and note buyers. These are rock solid, secure real estate notes that you can create on deals in your local area.

ABOUT THE AUTHOR

John Alexander is an active real estate investor of over 30-years and a best-selling author. He has trained tens of thousands of real estate investors nationally since 1994. He has authored over 10 books on various real estate flipping techniques including the creation and publication of the Flex Option, The Inverse Purchase, and the Compound Deed flip methods, the Contract Release, as well as various creative note buying methods.

www.JohnAlexander.com

Made in United States
North Haven, CT
30 May 2025